All scripture quotations, unless otherwise indicated, are taken from the King James Version of the Bible

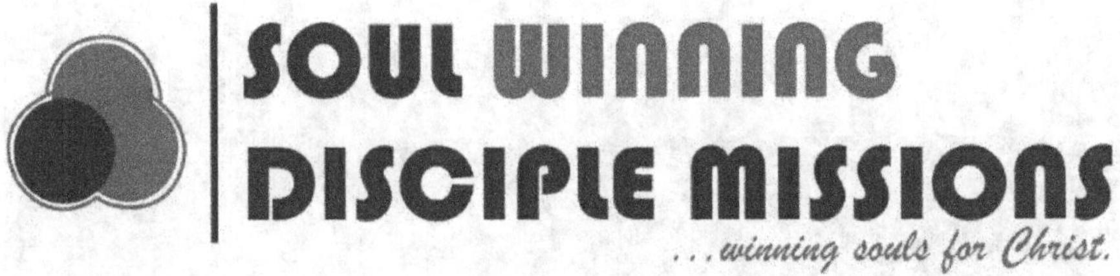

Off Access School road, School 2, Ilaro, Ogun State. Nigeria.

t.me/Soulwinningbelieverschurch

CONTENTS

FOREWORD

The importance of having a clear understanding of what exactly the Christian faith is all about can never be over emphasized. Many times, in many quarters, the facts of the Christian faith are mixed up with traditions of men and human philosophy, (Col.2:8). The implication of this, is that the Word of God is "made of none effect", (Matt.15:4-9) and the believers raised with such teachings will have distorted knowledge of God and a wrong identity of themselves. Christianity is built upon certain definite and unchanging truths - "The realities of Christianity", which every believer in Christ must learn, believe and build his/her conviction upon (Col.2:6-7).

The leadership of the local church has the responsibility, the mandate from God, to ensure the newly converted and every Christ's disciple be established in these truths and be able to teach the same to others, (2Tim.2:2).

I strongly believe and affirm that the information is this book is the exact, correct diet needed to ensure clear understanding of the realities of the Christian faith which guarantees systematic and steady spiritual growth for every believer.

The style of writing is simple, detailed and easy to understand with well explained biblical references. I recommend this material for Pastors, church leaders and everyone involved in disciple making, to be used as a basic tool for raising new converts and establishment of the saints in every local church. May the eyes of your understanding be enlightened as you feast on these timeless and precious truth.

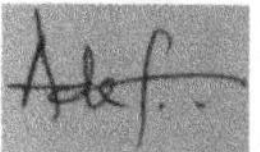

Sam. Gbenga Adefolu.

Pastor, Latter Glory Gospel Mission Int'l,

Ilaro, Ogun State, Nigeria.

ACKNOWLEDGEMENTS

I extend my deepest gratitude, and thanks to Rev. Chris Olusegun Onayinka, who I hold in high esteem as he has been the greatest influence in my life, and ministry. This book is a product of his immense labour over me (us) in word, and in doctrine.

Words fail, at this moment, to express my appreciation to my Pastor; Pastor Gbenga Adefolu, for his fatherly care, his immense love for me, and his unwavering support for me, and my ministry.

I cannot but appreciate all my mentors, friends, colleagues, partners in ministry, and my associates at SWBC and SWDM for their continued love, and their support.

Lastly, I appreciate my family for their unalloyed love and support. Thank you for being my biggest cheerleaders, I am grateful and I do not take you all for granted.

PREFACE

Having received Christ as your Lord and saviour, there are certain fundamental facts, of that experience, that the believer must be informed about. They are the reality of what has happened and what is expected of the believer.

This book seeks to present, in its simplest form, information about these basic realities of the Christian faith.

So sit back, get your Bible and your jotting materials, as we look through the scriptures together to study the "Realities of Christianity".

It's our hope that as you study through this material, your mind will be opened, your heart will be reassured of the love and the mercy of God in his salvation, and you will further be established in the Christian faith.

INTRODUCTION

Christianity is a reality and there are certain irrefutable truths that defines its practice, which the believer must understand.

The practice of Christianity is such that must stem from the written word and not mere assumptions or opinions else we will have a wrong practice of the faith, and where there is a wrong view or belief, there will be a wrong practice.

Every Scripture is inspired by God and is useful for teaching, for convincing, for correction of error, and for instruction in right doing;
- 2 Timothy 3:16 (Weymouth New Testament)

Where Christianity is concerned, the scriptures remain our teaching material and the basis for our convictions and practices.

There are folks who practice Judaism and other unchristian "traditions" today in the name of Christianity as a result of either negligence or misinterpretation of the written word(scriptures), hence our practice of Christianity must be based on the truth of God's word.

This presuppose that a bible teacher/believer must be diligent with the scriptures to ensure an accurate interpretation and understanding of the same because a careless interpretation can be injurious to his practice of Christianity, hence Paul instruction to Timothy;

[15] Study and do your best to present yourself to God approved, a workman [tested by trial] who has no reason to be ashamed, accurately handling and skillfully teaching the word of truth. 2 Timothy 2:15 (Amplified version)

The word associated with Christianity is Christian. A Christian is one who practice Christianity.

The word Christian is mentioned only three times in the Bible. The first mention of the word is seen in;

[26] *And when he had found him, he brought him unto Antioch. And it came to pass, that a whole year they assembled themselves with the church, and taught much people. And the disciples were called Christians first in Antioch.* - Acts 11:26

It is noteworthy that this was the first time believers were so called Christians.

The word Christian means "follower of Christ "

In Latin, the suffix -ian meant "the party of." A Christ-ian was "of the party of Jesus." It is like saying the "Jesus-ites," or "Jesus People," describing the people associated with Jesus Christ. There are other instances in scriptures where we will see similar cases;

[9] Then saith the woman of Samaria unto him, How is it that thou,

being a Jew, askest drink of me, which am a woman of Samaria? for the Jews have no dealings with the Samaritans.

[45] Then when he was come into Galilee, the Galilaeans received him, having seen all the things that he did at Jerusalem at the feast: for they also went unto the feast. - John 4:9,45

Notice, the use of the suffix - an to describe the people associated with a particular location; samaria- samaritans, Gallilee - Galilaeans. It is also on this premise the disciples were so called Christ-ians by the people of Antioch.

The name did not originate with Christ disciples, there were certain phrase used to describe them before they were referred to as Christians in Antioch.

*[15] And in those days Peter stood up in the midst of the **disciples**, and said, (the number of names together were about an hundred and twenty,)* - Acts 1:15

Luke in his record describe believers to as disciples and they are other several instances of such;

*[1] And in those days, when the number of the **disciples** was multiplied, there arose a murmuring of the Grecians against the Hebrews, because their widows were neglected in the daily ministration.*

*[2] Then the twelve called the multitude of the **disciples** unto them, and said, It is not reason that we should leave the word of God, and serve tables.*

*[7] And the word of God increased; and the number of the **disciples** multiplied in Jerusalem greatly; and a great company of the priests were obedient to the faith.* - Acts 6:1-2,7

*[1] And Saul, yet breathing out threatenings and slaughter against the **disciples** of the Lord, went unto the high priest,* - Acts 9:1

Believers were also called brethren

*[3] Wherefore, **brethren**, look ye out among you seven men of honest report, full of the Holy Ghost and wisdom, whom we may appoint over this business.* - Acts 6:3

*[1] And the apostles and **brethren** that were in Judaea heard that the Gentiles had also received the word of God.*

*[29] Then the **disciples**, every man according to his ability, determined to send relief unto the **brethren** which dwelt in Judaea:* - Acts 11:1,29

Believers were also called saints

*[13] Then Ananias answered, Lord, I have heard by many of this man, how much evil he hath done to thy **saints** at Jerusalem:*

*[32] And it came to pass, as Peter passed throughout all quarters, he came down also to the **saints** which dwelt at Lydda.* - Acts 9:13,32

The name did not originate from Jesus or His disciples. History has it that Antioch, arguably were famous for their readiness to jeer and call names, perhaps the opponents of Christianity in Antioch call Christ disciples Christians to mock and criticize the followers of Jesus as acting just like that Jesus of Nazareth who claimed to be the Christ. The name was never intended to be a "compliment", the church later adopted this name for themselves and used it to describe themselves as early as the second century A.D.

Other mention of the word Christian

[16] Yet if any man suffer as a Christian, let him not be ashamed; but let him glorify God on this behalf. - 1 Peter 4:16

Peter here spoke on the Christian sufferings, encouraging his audience to stand unashamed of the sufferings of Christ.

Obviously some are suffering because they are identified as Christians. This shows that the name had become very widely used, so much so that one could be persecuted for being numbered as a Christian.

[28] Then Agrippa said unto Paul, Almost thou persuadest me to be a Christian. - Acts 26:28

Paul in his defense before king Agrippa almost persuaded him to become a Christian. What was the persuasion about?

[22] Having therefore obtained help of God, I continue unto this day, witnessing both to small and great, saying none other things than those which the prophets and Moses did say should come:

[23] That Christ should suffer, and that he should be the first that should rise from the dead, and should shew light unto the people, and to the Gentiles.

[27] King Agrippa, believest thou the prophets? I know that thou believest.

[28] Then Agrippa said unto Paul, almost thou persuadest me to be a Christian. - Acts 26:22-23,27-28

The persuasion was about Christ's work of redemption as promised in the utterances of the prophets (the Old Testament scriptures), it was about the sufferings of Christ and the glory that will follow.

[10] Regarding this salvation, the prophets who prophesied about the grace [of God] that was intended for you, searched carefully and inquired [about this future way of salvation], [11] seeking to find out what person or what time the Spirit of Christ within them was indicating as He foretold the sufferings of Christ and the glories [destined] to follow. - 1 Peter 1:10-11 [amplified]

[26] Ought not Christ to have suffered these things, and to enter into his glory? [27] And beginning at Moses and all the prophets, he expounded unto them in all the scriptures the things concerning himself. [44] And he said unto them, these are the words which I spake unto you, while I was yet with you, that all things must be

fulfilled, which were written in the law of Moses, and in the prophets, and in the psalms, concerning me. - Luke 24:26-27,44

The scriptural texts above revealed that the utterances of the prophets were about Christ (His work of redemption, the salvation plan of God), hence Paul asked king Agrippa, if he believed the prophet, because he knew that if Agrippa did believe the words of the prophets, it will lead him to believe upon Jesus. He wanted to connect what Agrippa already believed to what he should believe.

This suggest that faith in Christ (work of redemption) is what makes a man a Christian.

That presupposes that Christianity is founded on Christ's work of salvation/redemption as revealed in the written word.

The message of Christ work of redemption is what the scriptures referred to as the gospel which bring about salvation.

[16] For I am not ashamed of the gospel of Christ: for it is the power of God unto salvation to every one that believeth; to the Jew first, and also to the Greek. - Romans 1:16

We will find in the book of act the content of the gospel the Apostles preached, as they persuade men into "Christianity".

[29] Men and brethren, let me freely speak unto you of the patriarch David, that he is both dead and buried, and his sepulchre is with us unto this day.

[30] Therefore being a prophet, and knowing that God had sworn with an oath to him, that of the fruit of his loins, according to the flesh, he would raise up Christ to sit on his throne;

[31] He seeing this before spake of the resurrection of Christ, that his

soul was not left in hell, neither his flesh did see corruption.

[32] This Jesus hath God raised up, whereof we all are witnesses.

[41] Then they that gladly received his word were baptized: and the same day there were added unto them about three thousand souls. - Acts 2:29-32,41

Just like Paul before Agrippa, Peter was teaching from the scriptures of the prophets;

[10] For thou wilt not leave my soul in hell; neither wilt thou suffer thine Holy One to see corruption. - Psalm 16:10

Peter made it clear that David prophesied about Christ resurrection to further affirm his testimony of the same.

We will find similar cases in the texts of scriptures below;

[18] But those things, which God before had shewed by the mouth of all his prophets, that Christ should suffer, he hath so fulfilled.

[19] Repent ye therefore, and be converted, that your sins may be blotted out, when the times of refreshing shall come from the presence of the Lord;

[20] And he shall send Jesus Christ, which before was preached unto you:

[25] Ye are the children of the prophets, and of the covenant which God made with our fathers, saying unto Abraham, And in thy seed shall all the kindreds of the earth be blessed. [26] Unto you first God, having raised up his Son Jesus, sent him to bless you, in turning away every one of you from his iniquities. - Acts 3:18-20,25-26

[10] Be it known unto you all, and to all the people of Israel, that by the name of Jesus Christ of Nazareth, whom ye crucified, whom God raised from the dead, even by him doth this man stand here before you whole. - Acts 4:10

[30] The God of our fathers raised up Jesus, whom ye slew and

hanged on a tree. [31] Him hath God exalted with his right hand to be a Prince and a Saviour, for to give repentance to Israel, and forgiveness of sins. - Acts 5:30-31

[39] And we are witnesses of all things which he did both in the land of the Jews, and in Jerusalem; whom they slew and hanged on a tree:

[40] Him God raised up the third day, and shewed him openly;

[42] And he commanded us to preach unto the people, and to testify that it is he which was ordained of God to be the Judge of quick and dead.

[43] To him give all the prophets witness, that through his name whosoever believeth in him shall receive remission of sins. - Acts 10:39-40,42-43

Like Paul's focused on Christ suffering (death) and resurrection, in his defence before king Agrippa (Acts 26:23), also the gospel preached in the book of acts was about Christ suffering and his glory (resurrection), as they persuade men to becoming a Christian.

Paul in his letter to Corinth, further summarizes the gospel in the events of the cross; Christ sufferings and glorification as prophesied in the scriptures of the prophets (Old Testament)

[1] Moreover, brethren, I declare unto you the gospel which I preached unto you, which also ye have received, and wherein ye stand;

[2] By which also ye are saved, if ye keep in memory what I preached unto you, unless ye have believed in vain.

[3] For I delivered unto you first of all that which I also received, how that Christ died for our sins according to the scriptures;

[4] And that he was buried, and that he rose again the third day

according to the scriptures: - 1 Corinthians 15:1-4

Hence, the essence of Christianity will be woven around this fact and details. It hinges on Christ work of redemption and salvation.

Christianity is therefore what Christ has done.

This makes it critical for every Christian to have a full grasp and recognition of the effects of what Christ accomplished for him in the resurrection.

[4] I always thank my God when I pray for you, Philemon,

[5] because I keep hearing about your faith in the Lord Jesus and your love for all of God's people.

[6] And I am praying that you will put into action the generosity that comes from your faith as you understand and experience all the good things we have in Christ. - Philemon 1:4-6 (New Living Translation)

Paul's prayer focus for Philemon here made it crystal clear that Christianity is practiced by knowledge and to the extent to which a believer understands all the good things he has in Christ, the realities of what Christ has accomplished for him is to the extent to which he will experience a fruitful Christian life.

This further affirm that Christian maturity will come by knowledge. Peter lends credence to this in his letter

[18] Let the gift of undeserved grace and the understanding that come from our Lord and Savior Jesus Christ help you keep on growing. Praise Jesus now and forever! Amen. - 2 Peter 3:18 (Contemporary English Version)

Believer will keep growing by his understanding of all that he has in Christ, which presuppose that once a man receives Christianity by faith in the gospel, the next thing is to subject his mind to the teaching of the word so that he will grow.

[2] As newborn babes, desire the sincere milk of the word, that ye may grow thereby: - 1 Peter 2:2

The word of God is the diet for the Christian growth. Peter here addressed the believer's attitude and attention to his growth in that he must keep having a child-like attitude to the word, he must stay desirous like an infant is desirous of his mother's breast. Hence, the believer must hold the word of God in high esteem and since he received Christianity by the word, he is to continue the practice by the word also.

Further in this study we will delve much more into the realities of all that Christ accomplished for the believers and how this affects the believers practice of Christianity.

CHAPTER ONE

WHAT DOES IT MEAN TO BE SAVED?

Salvation is what happens to a man upon believing the Gospel; which is how that Christ died for our sins and rose again on the third day for our justification, according to the scriptures. Faith in this simple fact is what saves a man.

[1] Moreover, brethren, I declare unto you the gospel which I preached unto you, which also ye have received, and wherein ye stand;

[2] By which also ye are saved, if ye keep in memory what I preached unto you, unless ye have believed in vain.

[3] For I delivered unto you first of all that which I also received, how that Christ died for our sins according to the scriptures;

[4] And that he was buried, and that he rose again the third day according to the scriptures:

- 1 Corinthians 15:1 - 4

Salvation is a hundred percent God's work, God accomplished the work of salvation and offered it to man freely. Where salvation is concerned, man's only role is to receive, by faith that which God has accomplished, nothing else is demanded from man to be saved.

But I will sacrifice unto thee with the voice of thanksgiving; I will pay that that I have vowed. ***Salvation is of the LORD*** - Jonah 2:9

God is the giver of salvation and he has made this gift available to every man (Titus 1:9) by delivering up his son, Jesus Christ, to die for the sins of the world and today, every man who believes in that very act is saved. This is what differentiates a believer from an unbeliever – faith in this Gospel.

For God so loved the world, that he gave his only begotten Son, that whosoever believeth in him should not perish, but have everlasting life. - John 3:16

The gospel that brings about salvation is very specific, salvation does not come just by believing in one God or believing that God exist, there is nothing special about that, Satan also believes there is one God.

Thou believest that there is one God; thou doest well: the devils also believe, and tremble. - James 2:19

What brings about salvation is faith in Jesus Christ, specifically, it is believing what he did to sin; how that he remit sins by sacrificing himself. (John 1:29, 1 john 2:1-2)

[8] But what saith it? The word is nigh thee, even in thy mouth, and in thy heart: that is, the word of faith, which we preach;

[9] That if thou shalt confess with thy mouth the Lord Jesus, and shalt believe in thine heart that God hath raised him from the dead, thou shalt be saved.

[10] For with the heart man believeth unto righteousness; and with the mouth confession is made unto salvation. - Romans 10:8 - 10

Similar to our index scriptural text, Paul's emphasis here,

on how to receive God's salvation, is to believe in Christ's resurrection. Definitely, no one will claim to believe Christ was raised and not believe he actually died.

Having seen this, we will examine briefly, **what, exactly, it is a man needs salvation from?**

And she shall bring forth a son, and thou shalt call his name JESUS: for he shall save his people from their sins. - Matthew 1:21

This is a faithful saying, and worthy of all acceptation, that Christ Jesus came into the world to save sinners; of whom I am chief. - 1Timothy 1:15

The above scriptural texts make it crystal clear that Christ's primary mission on the earth was to save people from their sins. Christ came for sinners (Luke 19:10, Matthew 15:24). This presumes that the salvation Jesus seeks to offer is from sins and, by extension, its effect; death.

for the wages of sin is death but the gift of God is eternal life through Jesus Christ our Lord. – Romans 6:23

The Scriptures revealed Christ as the savior from sins (Luke 2:11, John 4:42, Acts 5:31). No man has the ability to hold on to that office because no man can get himself saved from sins. That office of "The Saviour" exclusively belongs to Jesus. His job description is to save sinners from their sins. For a sinner to now come to Jesus for salvation and not be saved implies that Jesus is incapable and all his claims, and the prophets of old, are fallacious, which again questions the integrity of God.

That by two immutable things in which it was impossible for God to lie, we might have a strong consolation, who have fled for refuge to lay hold upon the hope set before us - Hebrew 6:18

In hope of eternal life, which God that cannot lie, promised before the world began – Titus 1:2

God has integrity, He cannot lie. He has a track record of always keeping his word. The incarnation and resurrection of Christ is enough proof that God keeps his words.

[18] But as God is true, our word towards you was not yea and nay

[19] For the son of God, Jesus Christ, who was preached among you by us, even by me and silvanus and Timotheus, was not yea and nay, but in him was yea.

[20] For all the promises of God in him are yea, and in him amen, unto the glory of God by us. – 2 Corinthians 1:18-20

In Christ's incarnation and resurrection, we find the fulfilment of God's promises reiterated through several of his prophets at different dispensations and ages, which further reinforces the integrity of God.

And he said unto them, These are the words which i spake unto you, while I was yet with you, that all things must be fulfilled, which were written in the law of moses, and in the prophets, and in the psalms, concerning me. -Luke 24:44

Apostle Paul, in his epistle, spoke of the state of the man who is without Christ or salvation as being dead in trespasses and sins.

[1] *And you hath he quickened, who were dead in trespasses and sins;*

[2] Wherein in time past ye walked according to the course of this world, according to the prince of the power of the air, the spirit that now worketh in the children of disobedience:

[3] Among whom also we all had our conversation in times past in the lusts of our flesh, fulfilling the desires of the flesh and of the mind; and were by nature the children of wrath, even as others. - Ephesians 2:1 - 3

The unsaved man is spiritually dead and thus requires a revival or quickening from the dead, which salvation provides.

When an unsaved man acknowledges Christ as his lord and saviour, he is raised back to life spiritually.

We have earlier established that salvation is deliverance from sin, and we will still not be wrong to assert that salvation is also the quickening of a man from spiritual death to life eternal.

For the wages of sin is death; but the gift of God is eternal life through Jesus Christ our Lord. - Romans 6:23

The reward of sin is death, and Jesus died that death. Jesus on the cross identified with humanity; he died in our place. He was without sin all through his earthly walk, yet he was punished for the sin of humanity.

Seeing then that we have a great high priest, that is passed into heavens, Jesus the son of God , let us hold fast our profession.

For we have not an high priest which cannot be touched with the feeling of our infirmities, ***but was in all points tempted like as we are, yet without sin*** – Hebrews 4:14-15

The just recompense for sin is death (Romans 1:29-32) and every man who is guilty of sin is indebted to death/eternal damnation. Hence, Jesus' death was to satisfy the demands of sin. The sacrifice of Jesus paid off completely the demands of sin, which makes the believer free from sin. Hence, when a man acknowledges Christ's sacrifice, he is redeemed from sin and death, because Jesus' death and life have now become our death and our life.

The man in Christ is identified with all that Jesus did for sin because all that Christ did has been accrued to the believer's account. Christ's sacrifice therefore becomes the legal ground for the justification of the man in Christ.

Christ hath redeemed us from the curse of the law, being made a curse for us: for it is written, cursed is every one that hangeth on a tree: - Galatians 3:13

For he hath made him to be sin for us, who knew no sin; that we might be made the righteousness of God in him. – 2 Corinthians 5:21

There is an allegory/parable I often love to use to explain this reality:

A man was caught in the act of robbery and was to be prosecuted in the law court. The judge sentenced the culprit to three years in prison in accordance with the law, but the lawyer who stood in for the culprit pleaded his case and presented himself as a substitute for the culprit, seeking to be imprisoned on behalf of the culprit while the culprit was released. I know that sounds almost impossible in our world today, but then it explains what exactly Christ did for humanity. It is called "the gospel," news that's too good to be true (believe). God's love for humanity expressed through Christ is indeed overwhelming.

The substitionary act of Christ has now become the legal

ground for the believer to be declared not guilty today, which makes Jesus the advocate of the believer.

[1] *My little children, these things write I unto you, that ye sin not.* ***And if any man sin, we have an advocate with the father, Jesus Christ the righteous:***

[2] And he is the propitiation for our sins: and not for ours only, but also for the sins of the whole world. – 1 John 2:1-2

Jesus's sacrifice makes available eternal life to humanity, which is to be received by faith in the gospel.

A man is said to have passed from death to life eternal, never to die again, simply by believing the gospel.

Verily, verily, I say unto you, He that heareth my word, and believeth on him that sent me, hath everlasting life, and shall not come into condemnation; but is passed from death unto life. - John 5:24

For God so loved the world, that he gave his only begotten Son, that whosoever believeth in him should not perish, but have everlasting life. - John 3:16

The texts of scripture above further reveal that eternal life is a possession that is received on earth by faith in the gospel. Eternal life is the proof of our salvation. It is not to be received after death, as purported by many. Eternal life is received on earth the moment a man believes the gospel. If a man does not have eternal life on earth, he definitely cannot have it in "heaven".

[9] If we receive the witness of men, the witness of God is greater: for this is the witness of God which he hath testified of his Son.

[10] He that believeth on the Son of God hath the witness in himself: he that believeth not God hath made him a liar; because he believeth not the record that God gave of his Son.

[11] And this is the record, that God hath given to us eternal life, and this life is in his Son.

[12] He that hath the Son hath life; and he that hath not the Son of God hath not life.

[13] These things have I written unto you that believe on the name of the Son of God; that ye may know that ye have eternal life, and that ye may believe on the name of the Son of God. – 1John 5:9-13

This means that the believer possesses eternal life, which is different from ordinary human life; it is a supernatural life; it is God's life or nature in a man. It is a quality of life. It is not just about living forever after death; it is the Spirit of Christ in a man. Apostle Paul often refers to it as 'Christ in you' in his epistles.

[9] But ye are not in the flesh, but in the Spirit, if so be that the Spirit of God dwell in you. Now if any man have not the Spirit of Christ, he is none of his.

[10] And if Christ be in you, the body is dead because of sin; but the Spirit is life because of righteousness. - Romans 8:9 - 10

Therefore, Christ in a man is eternal life in a man, and this is the proof of our salvation.

In whom ye also trusted, after that ye heard the word of truth, the gospel of your salvation: in whom also after that ye believed, ye were sealed with that holy Spirit of promise, - Ephesians 1:13

When a man receives the gospel, he partakes of the life of God.

According as his divine power hath given us all things that pertain unto life and godliness through the knowledge of him that hath called us to glory and virtue - 1 peter 1:3

In His conversation with Nicodemus, Jesus introduced a term that describes the reality of the man who accepts his gospel: BORN AGAIN, which he further defined as being born of the Spirit.

[4] Nicodemus saith unto him, how can a man be born when he is old? can he enter the second time into his mother's womb, and be born?

[5] Jesus answered, Verily, verily, I say unto thee, except a man be born of water and of the Spirit, he cannot enter into the kingdom of God.

[6] That which is born of the flesh is flesh; and that which is born of the Spirit is spirit. - John 3:4 - 6

It is noteworthy to see that Jesus made a dichotomy between the natural birth, which he called being born of the flesh, and the spiritual birth, which he called being born of the Spirit. This further explains being born again as a spiritual birth, a spiritual reality.

The word "born again" implies being born anew or being born from above, and this brings to the fore a parental involvement, however different from that of the flesh, so the "again" there is not in reference to being born the second time like Nicodemus assumed, rather it is to explain a new beginning or new birth from a new source, which is the Spirit.

[4] Nicodemus saith unto him, how can a man be born when he is old? can he enter the second time into his mother's womb, and be born?

[5] Jesus answered, Verily, verily, I say unto thee, except a man be born of water and of the Spirit, he cannot enter into the kingdom of God. - John 3:4-5

Jesus explained being born again as being born of the Spirit, pointing to the fact that the man in Christ is in a father-to-child relationship with God. To be born of the Spirit is, therefore, to be born of God.

God is a Spirit*: and they that worship him must worship him in spirit and in truth.* - John 4:24

Whosoever believeth that Jesus is the Christ is ***born of God*** *: and everyone that loveth him that begat loveth him also that is begotten of him.* – 1 John 5:1

Jesus also used being born of water to explain the reality of this New birth.

Jesus answered, Verily, verily, I say unto thee, except a man be born of water and of the Spirit, he cannot enter into the kingdom of God. - John 3:5

Jesus simply used water to further explain what happens to the believer in the new birth experience as prophesied in the scriptures of the prophets.

[25] Then will I sprinkle clean water upon you, and ye shall be clean : from all your filthiness, and from all your idols, will I cleanse you.

[26] A new heart also will i give you, ***a new spirit will I put within you*** *: and I will take away the stony heart out of your flesh and will give you a heart of flesh*

[27] And I will ***put my spirit within you****, and cause you to walk in*

my statutes, and ye shall keep my judgments and do them. - Eze 36:25-27

Prophetically, Ezekiel spoke of the Spirit God would put in man, and this he referred to as God sprinkling water to cleanse men, which explains that in the new birth, man receives God's spirit within him and is thus made holy and cleansed by that Spirit received. This was further explained in clear terms in the letter of the Apostles.

And such were some of you: but ye are washed, but ye are sanctified, but ye are justified in the name of the Lord Jesus, and by the Spirit of our God. - 1 Corinthian 6:11

Not by works of righteousness which we have done, but according to his mercy he saved us, by the washing of regeneration, and renewing of the Holy Ghost; -Titus 3:5

So, by faith in the gospel, a man becomes born again, receives the Spirit of God, and is thus made holy by that Spirit he received. This is the same thing Jesus was explaining in John 3.

For God so loved the world that he gave his only begotten son that whosoever believeth in him should not perish but have everlasting life – John 3: 16

Jesus explained being born again or being born of the spirit as receiving everlasting life. A further study of the book of John revealed that what Jesus meant by "receiving eternal life" was receiving the Spirit, similar to Ezekiel's prophecy and the explanation of the Apostles in their epistles.

[10] Jesus answered and said unto her, If thou knewest the gift of

God, and who it is that saith to thee, Give me to drink; thou wouldest have asked of him, and he would have given thee living water.

[11] The woman saith unto him, Sir, thou hast nothing to draw with, and the well is deep: from whence then hast thou that living water?

[12] Art thou greater than our father Jacob, which gave us the well, and drank thereof himself, and his children, and his cattle?

[13] Jesus answered and said unto her, Whosoever drinketh of this water shall thirst again:

[14] But whosoever drinketh of the water that I shall give him shall never thirst; but the water that I shall give him shall be in him a well of water springing up into everlasting life. - John 4:10-14

Jesus is again using the word "water" similar to Ezekiel's usage of the word, which is about the Spirit God will give to man, which will clean and make man a new creation. This is the same thing that Jesus is saying to the Samaritan woman.

He spoke of a living water (water of life) which he will give man to drink and will quench man's thirst forever. He further explained that the water will spring up unto everlasting life. This is a description of the Spirit of life, which is himself, which will be given to man in his resurrection.

[33] For the bread of God is he which cometh down from heaven, and giveth life unto the world.

[34] Then said they unto him, Lord, evermore give us this bread.

[35] And Jesus said unto them, I am the bread of life: he that cometh to me shall never hunger; and he that believeth on me shall never thirst. - John 6:33-35

Here, again, Jesus mentioned a living bread of God (bread of life) that will satisfy men's hunger and thirst. A further study revealed that to partake of the bread is to believe in him.

[33] For the bread of God is he which cometh down from heaven, and giveth life unto the world.

[34] Then said they unto him, Lord, evermore give us this bread.

[35] And Jesus said unto them, I am the bread of life: he that cometh to me shall never hunger; and he that believeth on me shall never thirst.

[51] I am the living bread which came down from heaven: if any man eat of this bread, he shall live for ever: and the bread that I will give is my flesh, which I will give for the life of the world. - John 6:33-35,51

Partaking of the bread is what He now later refer to as eating his flesh and drinking his blood.

[53] Then Jesus said unto them, Verily, verily, I say unto you, Except ye eat the flesh of the Son of man, and drink his blood, ye have no life in you.

[54] Whoso eateth my flesh, and drinketh my blood, hath eternal life; and I will raise him up at the last day.

[55] For my flesh is meat indeed, and my blood is drink indeed.

[56] He that eateth my flesh, and drinketh my blood, dwelleth in me, and I in him.

[57] As the living Father hath sent me, and I live by the Father: so he that eateth me, even he shall live by me.

[58] This is that bread which came down from heaven: not as your fathers did eat manna, and are dead: he that eateth of this bread shall live for ever. - John 6:53-58

Jesus was playing with words here yet explaining the same concept. Recall, He had earlier referred to himself as the living bread, which a man would eat and live forever, which we have seen speak of faith in him. Later on, he replaced "eating the living bread of God" with "eating his flesh and drinking his blood," which still explains the same concept— However, Jesus technically brings to the fore here his sacrificial offering for sins, pointing his audience's attention to what will be fulfilled on the cross. Thus, to eat the living bread of God is to eat his flesh and drink his blood, which is to believe specifically in the event of his crucifixion, his sacrificial offering for sins. Hence, he stated in verse 51 that the bread He will give for the life of the world is his flesh. So whatever Jesus is teaching here will be futuristic and not available at that time because he was not yet crucified.

It is also important to note that Jesus was teaching from the scriptures of the prophet, as his custom was.

[15] And when the children of Israel saw it, they said one to another, It is manna: for they wist not what it was. And Moses said unto them, This is the bread which the LORD hath given you to eat.

[16] This is the thing which the LORD hath commanded, Gather of it every man according to his eating, an omer for every man, according to the number of your persons; take ye every man for them which are in his tents.

[17] And the children of Israel did so, and gathered, some more, some less.

[18] And when they did mete it with an omer, he that gathered much had nothing over, and he that gathered little had no lack; they gathered every man according to his eating. - Exodus 16:15-18

Jesus taught from this event in the wilderness. Obviously, his audience, being Jews, were familiar with it. Hence, Jesus referred to the men who ate of this bread as their fathers. He described it as a shadow which points to him.

[31] Our fathers did eat manna in the desert; as it is written, He gave them bread from heaven to eat.

[32] Then Jesus said unto them, Verily, verily, I say unto you, Moses gave you not that bread from heaven; but my Father giveth you the true bread from heaven.

[33] For the bread of God is he which cometh down from heaven, and giveth life unto the world

- John 6:31-33

The manna (bread) God gave the children of Israel in the wilderness points to Jesus. When they ate it, it did not quench their hunger and thirst forever; it only provided a temporal satisfaction that could not be the true bread of God.

The true bread of God is Christ. He offers eternal life, a permanent and eternal satisfaction. He quenches man's hunger and thirst forever.

And Jesus said unto them, I am the bread of life: he that cometh to me shall never hunger; and he that believeth on me shall never thirst.
- John 6:35

So, when a man comes to Jesus, he is offered a living water and a living bread. This is Jesus' way of saying he offers eternal/ everlasting life, the Spirit of life to all who believe in him.

This is the same truth the Apostles taught in their epistles:

*[9] But ye are not in the flesh, but in the Spirit, if so be that the **Spirit of God** dwell in you. Now if any man have not the **Spirit of Christ**, he is none of his.*

*[10] And if Christ be in you, the body is dead because of sin; but the **Spirit is life** because of righteousness.*

*[14] For as many as are led by the **Spirit of God**, they are the sons of God*

*[15] For ye have not received the Spirit of bondage again to fear; but ye have received the **Spirit of adoption,** whereby we cry, Abba, Father* - Romans 8:9-10, 14-15

Noteworthy are the terminologies Apostle Paul used to describe the word "Spirit"—"the Spirit of God, the Spirit of Christ, the Spirit is (of) life, the Spirit of Adoption." All these terms are used by the Apostle Paul to describe the Spirit the believer receives when he believes the gospel. However, they are all the same Spirit. This presupposes that the Spirit of life is the Spirit of Christ, which is the Spirit of adoption, and this is to explain the characters of the Spirit in the believer: how that the Spirit of God in the believer is Christ in the believer, which is (eternal) life in the believer, by which the believer has been adopted as sons of God and can thus refer to God as a Father. The Spirit indwelling the believer is how Paul explained the believers' union with God in Christ, similar to Jesus in the synoptic gospels.

Paul also made it clear that every man without the Spirit of Christ is alien to this reality of man's union with God in Christ, such a man is alien to God; he is not a part of God's family. This is the reality of those who have yet to accept the gospel.

[37] In the last day, that great day of the feast, Jesus stood and cried, saying, If any man thirst, let him come unto me, and drink.

[38] He that believeth on me, as the scripture hath said, out of his belly shall flow rivers of living water.

[39] (But this spake he of the Spirit, which they that believe on him should receive: for the Holy Ghost was not yet given; because that Jesus was not yet glorified.) - John 7: 37–39

Here again, Jesus spoke of the spirit he would give to those who believe in his resurrection and glorification.

Similar to Jesus' explanation to the Samaritan woman in John 4, Jesus here again taught from the scriptures of the prophet and very specifically Ezekiel's prophecy, as we have earlier seen. Hence, to drink would be to believe in him, and "rivers of living water" speaks of the Spirit which will be given and will consequently make man clean and a new creation, while the phrase "his belly" would bring to mind the event of Jonah in the belly of the fish. As you recall, Jesus had the custom of teaching from the scriptures of the prophets.

[25] Then he said unto them, O fools, and slow of heart to believe all that the prophets have spoken:

[26] Ought not Christ to have suffered these things, and to enter into his glory?

[27] ***And beginning at Moses and all the prophets, he expounded unto them in all the scriptures the things concerning himself.***

[44] And he said unto them, These are the words which I spake unto you, while I was yet with you, that all things must be fulfilled, which were written in the law of Moses, and in the prophets, and in the psalms, concerning me.

[45] Then opened he their understanding, that they might understand the scriptures, - Luke 24:25-27,44-45

The texts of scriptures above further corroborate the fact that Jesus had a custom of teaching from the Scriptures of the Prophets (Genesis to Malachi). For the first time after his resurrection, Jesus had what we can call a Bible study with his disciples here, and Luke records that he taught them things about himself, specifically his sufferings and the glory that will follow, which explains the facts surrounding his death, burial, and resurrection, and this he taught systemically, beginning from Moses and all the prophets.

A closer look at verse 44 reveals that when Jesus said, beginning with Moses and all the prophets, it implies He began teaching about himself from the writings of Moses, which are Genesis to Deuteronomy, the writings of the prophets, and the psalms, all of which are encapsulated in what we now call the Old Testament Scriptures, even though Jesus and the Apostles never called them that.

Worthy of note, also, is that Jesus further affirms that what He taught them before his crucifixion, that is, while He was with them in the flesh, was not any different from what He had just opened their understanding to see from the Scriptures, which will mean that the synoptic gospels (Matthew-John), where we have the sermons of Jesus before his crucifixion recorded, some of which we have explored, will be explaining the same thing Jesus opened the minds of his disciples to see from the scriptures after his resurrection, following the same systematic approach of explaining the scriptures.

Hence, we are going to find the background of Jesus' sermons in the four gospels, in the scriptures of the prophets.

<u>Back to John 7:37-39</u>

In the last day, that great day of the feast, Jesus stood and cried, saying, If any man thirst, let him come unto me, and drink.

He that believeth on me, as the scripture hath said, out of his belly shall flow rivers of living water.

(But this spake he of the Spirit, which they that believe on him should receive: for the Holy Ghost was not yet given; because that Jesus was

not yet glorified.) - John 7: 37–39

The phrase out of his belly here brings to mind the event of Jonah in the belly of the fish.

Now the LORD had prepared a great fish to swallow up Jonah. And Jonah was in the belly of the fish three days and three nights. - Jonah 1:17

Jonah was in the belly of the fish for three days and three nights, just like Jesus would later be in the grave for three days and three nights, this events therefore will be pointing to Jesus' crucifixion and experience in the grave.

Jesus also referenced this event in Matthew

For as Jonas was three days and three nights in the whale's belly; so shall the Son of man be three days and three nights in the heart of the earth. - Matthew 12:40

Recall, Jesus' audience were Jews who were familiar with this event, so these folks should understand what he meant when he used that phrase "out of his belly", he was simply making reference to his crucifixion, his sufferings which will be like that of Jonah.

Therefore, that statement by Jesus "out of his belly shall flow the rivers of living waters" was Jesus' way of pointing his audience's attention to his Crucifixion, how that from his crucifixion and consequent resurrection will his Spirit be given, which is his life or himself.

Jesus is still repeating the same thing he taught from John 3 to 6 here.

He was teaching about what his sufferings and consequent

glorification will offer the man who believes in him using the same systematic approach of explaining from the scriptures of the prophets.

Recall that we have earlier established that when a man comes to Christ, he will be offered eternal/everlasting life, which is the Spirit of life or the Spirit of Christ or Christ in the believer, and this is what salvation is about.

In whom ye also trusted, after that ye heard the word of truth, the gospel of your salvation: in whom also after that ye believed, ye were sealed with that holy Spirit of promise,

Which is the earnest of our inheritance until the redemption of the purchased possession, unto the praise of his glory. - Ephesians 1:13-14

Upon believing in the Gospel of salvation, a man is sealed with the Spirit of promise.

Spirit of promise simply refers to the Spirit indwelling the believer. It is the same thing as the Spirit of life prophesied in the Scriptures of the prophets, as earlier established.

To be sealed with the Spirit of promise implies that the Spirit received at salvation guarantees the salvation of the man. Hence, Paul further explained that the Spirit received is the down payment of our inheritance until the redemption of the purchased possession. Paul is making it clear that the Spirit indwelling the believer is the eternal security of his salvation. That is how God assures him that he has been saved and his body which is a part His purchased possession, will also be saved from corruption.

[9] But ye are not in the flesh, but in the Spirit, if so be that the Spirit of God dwell in you. Now if any man have not the Spirit of Christ, he is none of his.

[15] For ye have not received the spirit of bondage again to fear; but ye have received the Spirit of adoption, whereby we cry, Abba, Father.

[19] For the earnest expectation of the creature waiteth for the manifestation of the sons of God.

[20] For the creature was made subject to vanity, not willingly, but by reason of him who hath subjected the same in hope,

[21] Because the creature itself also shall be delivered from the bondage of corruption into the glorious liberty of the children of God.

[22] For we know that the whole creation groaneth and travaileth in pain together until now.

[23] And not only they, but ourselves also, which have the firstfruits of the Spirit, even we ourselves groan within ourselves, waiting for the adoption, to wit, the redemption of our body. - Romans 8:9,15,19-23

The texts of scripture above further corroborate the reality of the believers' hope of his bodily redemption/salvation from corruption. Worthy of note is Paul's reference to the indwelling Spirit received, upon salvation, as the first fruit of the Spirit and where there is first fruit there has to be further fruits. This alludes to the fact that the Spirit indwelling the believer, guarantees his hope of complete salvation.

Recall that Apostle Paul refers to the Spirit received at salvation as the promised Spirit; bringing to the fore the utterance/ scriptures of the prophets. Furthermore, in his other letters, he referred to this as eternal life which God promised before the world began.

In hope of eternal life, which God, that cannot lie, promised before the world began; - Titus 1:2

Paul, an apostle of Jesus Christ by the will of God, according to the promise of life which is in Christ Jesus, - 2 Timothy 1:1

This promised life is otherwise known as the "promised Spirit" which was made available for all men by the sacrifice of Jesus Christ. In the Old Testament, what they had was the promise of life which is the same as the promise of the Spirit; the promise of sonship or promise of the new birth.

Christ hath redeemed us from the curse of the law, being made a curse for us: for it is written, Cursed is every one that hangeth on a tree:

That the blessing of Abraham might come on the Gentiles through Jesus Christ; that we might receive the promise of the Spirit through faith. - Galatians 3:13 - 14

Now faith is the substance of things hoped for, the evidence of things not seen. - Hebrews 11:1

The writer of Hebrews spoke of the faith of the patriarchs as an action they were hoping for and evidence they have not seen, which relates to Christ and his work.

Looking unto Jesus the author and finisher of our faith; who for the joy that was set before him endured the cross, despising the shame, and is set down at the right hand of the throne of God. - Hebrews 12:2

The verse above speaks of Jesus as the author and finisher of their faith, therefore they lived in the faith of what Jesus will do. However, today, what they hoped for has been fulfilled in the resurrection of Jesus.

For all the promises of God in him are yea, and in him Amen, unto the glory of God by us. - 2 Corinthians1:20

Christ, having finished the work, sat at the right hand of the Father as a proof that the work is done!

Who being the brightness of his glory, and the express image of his person, and upholding all things by the word of his power, when he had by himself purged our sins, sat down on the right hand of the Majesty on high; - Hebrews 1:3

Therefore, the new birth, eternal life, the indwelling of the Spirit are available today and can be received by faith in the gospel. A man receives this and is also engrafted into the family of God as a Son.

For ye have not received the spirit of bondage again to fear; but ye have received the Spirit of adoption, whereby we cry, Abba, Father.

The Spirit itself beareth witness with our spirit, that we are the children of God. - Romans 8:15 - 16

And because ye are sons, God hath sent forth the Spirit of his Son into your hearts, crying, Abba, Father. - Galatians 4:6

This means that, upon believing the gospel, a man becomes born again. So, just as a man inevitably becomes someone's son via procreation in the natural, the same way a man receives the new birth, he inevitably becomes fathered by God; so faith in the gospel is how God procreates; that is how a man comes into union with God in Christ.

Being born again is therefore God's act, and not man's actions. As it is impossible for a child to exist without a parent, to be born again therefore is to partake of the life of God, which is the receiving of the Spirit. This explains the reality of the believers' union with God in Christ, which will be further explained in the proceeding chapter.

[2] Elect according to the foreknowledge of God the Father, through sanctification of the Spirit, unto obedience and sprinkling of the blood of Jesus Christ: Grace unto you, and peace, be multiplied.

[3] Blessed be the God and Father of our Lord Jesus Christ, which according to his abundant mercy hath begotten us again unto a lively hope by the resurrection of Jesus Christ from the dead, - 1Peter 1:2 - 3

Being born again, not of corruptible seed, but of incorruptible, by the word of God, which liveth and abideth forever. – 1 Peter 1:23

God has begotten us again, by His resurrection. Hence, the new birth is found in this resurrection. In the same way Christ was raised from the dead by the glory of the Father never to die again, the believer has also been raised from the dead by the glory of the Father never to die again. This implies that the new birth is our identification with Christ.

Therefore we are buried with him by baptism into death: that like as Christ was raised up from the dead by the glory of the Father, even so we also should walk in newness of life. - Romans 6:4

Jesus in His incarnation was called the only begotten of the

Father while in His resurrection He became the first begotten, the firstborn.

And the Word was made flesh, and dwelt among us, (and we beheld his glory, the glory as of the only begotten of the Father,) full of grace and truth. - John 1:14

And he is the head of the body, the church: who is the beginning, the ***firstborn from the dead****; that in all things he might have the preeminence.* - Colossians 1:18

The word firstborn implies a prototype; the prototype is a model of every other, meaning Jesus becoming the first begotten will imply there are other sons.

[10]For it became him, for whom are all things, and by whom are all things, in bringing many sons unto glory, to make the captain of their salvation perfect through sufferings.

[11]For both he that sanctifieth and they who are sanctified are all of one: for which cause he is not ashamed to call them brethren,

[13]And again, I will put my trust in him. And again, Behold I and the children which God hath given me. - Hebrews 2:10 – 11, 13

The children God has given him are a product of the resurrection of Christ, and in the resurrection, a man is identified with Christ when he believes the gospel. Hence, Christ is identified with man's state of sin and death (2 Corinthians 5:21), and when He rose from the dead, He defeated death.

Forasmuch then as the children are partakers of flesh and blood, he also himself likewise took part of the same; that through death he might destroy him that had the power of death, that is, the devil; - Hebrews 2:14

Hence, He became the "sample son" upon His resurrection, the model of sons raised from the dead; therefore, the glory of Christ in His resurrection is seen in the sons He brought into glory. This is where His kingdom began.

Who being the brightness of his glory, and the express image of his person, and upholding all things by the word of his power, when he had by himself purged our sins, sat down on the right hand of the Majesty on high; - Hebrews 1:3

But ye are come unto mount Sion, and unto the city of the living God, the heavenly Jerusalem, and to an innumerable company of angels, - Hebrews 12:22

The church is therefore referred to as the gathering in the firstborn; Christ Jesus is the prototype, the model of the New Man. Now we are identified with His resurrection life. Who He is, is who we are, where He is, that is where we are.

CHAPTER TWO

OUR IDENTIFICATION WITH CHRIST

We shall be examining briefly some of the words used to explain the believers' identification with Christ, which is predicated upon the sacrifice of Jesus for sin.

The Believer is a New Creation

Therefore if any man be in Christ, he is a new creature: old things are passed away; behold, all things are become new. - 2 Corinthians 5:17

The word "new creation" implies a new species or a new breed of man made in Christ. This is what Jesus referred to as being born again in John 3.

This newness is a result of the believers identification with Christ in his resurrection.

[4]Therefore we are buried with him by baptism into death: that like as Christ was raised up from the dead by the glory of the Father, even so we also should walk in newness of life.

[5]For if we have been planted together in the likeness of his death, we shall be also in the likeness of his resurrection:

[6]Knowing this, that our old man is crucified with him, that the

body of sin might be destroyed, that henceforth we should not serve sin.

[7]For he that is dead is freed from sin.

[8Now if we be dead with Christ, we believe that we shall also live with him: - Romans 6:4 - 8

The believer is a man in Christ. Hence, this is the believer's status and position, and to see otherwise is to wrongly see. Hence, the man in Christ is a new creature, and in "reality" he never existed until the new birth. He is newly born just like a new born baby; he is seen as though he never had a past of sins or wrongs. Hence, Apostle Paul used the word "behold" to call our attention to this important reality. That is, this is what should be focused on, the reality of that new beginning, all that God had done in Christ in the New Creature through His death, burial, and resurrection.

David and Ezekiel prophesied about this man.

This shall be written for the generation to come: and the people which shall be created shall praise the LORD. - Psalms 102:18

The word "generation to come" meant it was a future event, hence the generation to come are "the people that shall be created", and that word "created" will imply something that has no prior existence, hence he could not have been talking about the first Adam but a new species, a new kind of humanity in the last Adam (Christ).

[26] A new heart also will I give you, and a new spirit will I put within you: and I will take away the stony heart out of your flesh, and I will give you an heart of flesh.

[27]And I will put my spirit within you, and cause you to walk in my

statutes, and ye shall keep my judgments, and do them.

[28]And ye shall dwell in the land that I gave to your fathers; and ye shall be my people, and I will be your God. - Ezekiel 36:26 - 28

The term “new heart”, “new spirit”, “within you” all points to the new creature. Ezekiel was speaking ahead of time of the man in Christ, the new creature that based on their nature they will act on God’s word.

The Believer is Forgiven

In whom we have redemption through his blood, the forgiveness of sins, according to the riches of his grace; - Ephesians 1:7

Very vitally is to observe that forgiveness here is taught in past tense and it is taught as the work of grace predicated on the sacrifice of Jesus. It is given undeservedly and unconditionally through the blood of Jesus. So the believer has forgiveness of sins as a possession.

The word "forgiveness" as used by apostle Paul in the text above is a word that also implies remission, which explains the sending or taking away of our sins. This is what was accomplished in the sacrifice of Jesus. Hence, faith in Christ makes this a reality in a man’s life today.

My little children, these things write I unto you, that ye sin not. And if any man sin, we have an advocate with the Father, Jesus Christ the righteous

And he is the propitiation for our sins: and not for ours only, but also for the sins of the whole world.: - 1 John 2:1

The basis of forgiveness is the sacrifice of Jesus. The text above reveals Jesus as the offering for the sins of the world, and it is on this basis that forgiveness of sins is made available for all who believe. Hence, the believer has forgiveness of sins in Christ. Jeremiah spoke of this in prophecy;

[31]Behold, the days come, saith the LORD, that i will make a new covenant with the house of Israel, and the house of Judah:

[32]Not according to the covenant that I made with their fathers in the day that I took them by the hand to bring them out of the land of Egypt; which my covenant they brake, although I was an husband unto them, saiths the LORD:

[33]But this shall be the covenant that I will make with the house of Israel; after those days, saith the LORD, I will put my law in their inward parts, and write it in their hearts; and I will be their God and they shall be my people.

[34]And they shall teach no more every man his neighbour, and every man his brother, saying, Know the Lord: for all shall know me, from the least unto the greatest of them, Saith the LORD; for I will forgive their iniquity, and I will remember their sin no more. – Jeremiah 31:31-34

This is the New covenant fulfilled in Christ. The writer of Hebrews referenced this in Hebrews 8:10–12.

Ezekiel also prophesied about this in Ezekiel 36:26-28.

This covenant is about a nation and a family that God will establish on the earth in Christ; a forgiven and holy tribe of God on the earth where God will not count or remember sins. The new creation man is a citizen of that nation.

Now therefore ye are no more strangers and foreigners, but ***fellow citizens*** *with the saints, and of the* ***household of God;*** - Ephesians 2:19

But ye are a ***chosen generation, a royal priesthood, an holy nation, a peculiar people;*** *that ye should show forth the praises of him who hath called you out of darkness into his marvelous light* - 1 Peter 2:9

[22]But ye are come to mount zion, and unto the city of the living God, the heavenly Jerusalem, and to an innumerable company of angels,

[23]To the general assembly and the church of the firstborn, which are written in heaven, and to God the judge of all, and to the spirits of just men made perfect,

[24]And to Jesus the mediator of the new covenant, and to the blood of sprinkling, that speaketh better things than that of Abel. – Hebrews 12:22-24

The Man in Christ has come to that city of God where there is no remembrance of sins.

Under the law/old covenant, there was a remembrance of sins every year based on animal sacrifices, because those sacrifices were imperfect and could not take away sins.

[3But in those sacrifices there is a remembrance again made of sins every year.

[10]For by one offering he hath perfected for ever them that are sanctified. - Hebrews 10:3,14

But in the new covenant, the sacrifice for sins is perfect; it was done once and for all by the offering of Christ. Therefore, sins are forgiven, remitted, and taken away by the sacrifice of Jesus; hence, God has no remembrance or imputation of sins and iniquities to the believer. David prophesied this.

[1] Blessed is he whose transgression is forgiven, whose sin is covered.

[2]Blessed is the man unto whom the LORD imputeth not iniquity,

and in whose spirit there is no guile. - Psalms 32:1 - 2

David, speaking in prophecy concerning the new creation man referred to him as a blessed man because his transgression is forgiven, covered and will not be imputed upon him.

Apostle Paul and the rest of the Apostles lend credence to this also, they taught forgiveness of sins as Christ finished work and as a gift of God without conditions in their Epistles.

Saying,Blessed are they whose iniquities are forgiven, and whose sins are covered. - Romans 4:7

And be ye kind one to another, tenderhearted, forgiving one another, even as God for Christ's sake hath forgiven you. - Ephesians 4:32

And you, being dead in your sins and the uncircumcision of your flesh, hath he quickened together with him, having forgiven you all trespasses; - Colossians 2:13

I write unto you, little children, because your sins are forgiven you for his name's sake. - 1 John 2:12

The Believer is Saved and Redeemed

The word "redeem" is a word that means ransom; it implies a price paid for a man; hence the price is the man's value. The believer's redemption is in the blood of Jesus Christ. His blood is the price paid, and that is the value of His redemption.

For this is my blood of the new testament, which is shed for many for the remission of sins. - Matthew 26:28

Take heed therefore unto yourselves, and to all the flock, over the which the Holy Ghost hath made you overseers, to feed the church of God, which he hath purchased with his own blood. - Acts 20:28

[18]Forasmuch as ye know that ye were not redeemed with corruptible things, as silver and gold, from your vain conversation received by tradition from your fathers;

[19]But with the precious blood of Christ, as of a lamb without blemish and without spot: - 1 Peter 1:18 - 19

The blood of Christ refers to life of Jesus himself.

For the life of the flesh is in the blood: and I have given it to you upon the altar to make an atonement for your souls: for it is the blood that maketh an atonement for the soul.); - - Leviticus 17:11

Blood speaks of life. To offer blood is to offer life. Under the Old Testament, the high priest offers animal sacrifice for the atonement of the sins of himself and the children of Israel. They offer the blood of animals; bulls and goats, to atone for their sins. This explains that the animals' life is given on the alter for the atonement of their soul.

However, this sacrifice is imperfect as it is impossible for the blood of bulls and goats to take away sin. Hence, they offered this sacrifice year after year. In the same vein, Jesus Christ offered his blood, which is his life, for the atonement of our souls. So, in the New Testament, Jesus is both the sacrifice and our high priest.

[11]But Christ being come an high priest of good things to come, by a greater and more perfect tabernacle, not made with hands, that is to say, not of this building;

[12]Neither by the blood of goats and calves, but by his own blood he entered in once into the holy place, having obtained eternal

redemption for us.

[24]For Christ is not entered into the holy places made with hands, which are the figure of the true; but into heaven itself, now to appear in the presence of God for us - Hebrews 9:11 – 12, 24

By His blood, Jesus obtained eternal redemption for us. He shed his blood for us, not on Calvary as many assume. The scriptural texts above reveal that Jesus, being our high priest and our sacrifice for sins, entered into the holy place (heavenly) by his own blood (life) to obtain eternal redemption for us. He offered His blood and life for us in heaven, and after this, He sat down at the right hand of the Father as an eternal intercession and as proof that a believer is redeemed forever. So, unlike the Old Covenant where the high priests offer animal sacrifice year after year, the Christ Sacrifice is once for all. This presupposes that the perfection, sanctification, redemption, and all other blessings of God in Christ are received once and, as a result, eternal.

[1]For the law having a shadow of good things to come, and not the very image of the things, can never with those sacrifices which they offered year by year continually make the comers thereunto perfect.

[2]For then would they not have ceased to be offered? because that the worshippers once purged should have had no more conscience of sins.

[10]By the which will we are sanctified through the offering of the body of Jesus Christ once for all.

[11] every priest standeth daily ministering and offering oftentimes the same sacrifices, which can never take away sins:

[12]But this man, after he had offered one sacrifice for sins for ever, sat down on the right hand of God;

[13] From henceforth expecting till his enemies be made his footstool.

[14] For by one offering he hath perfected for ever them that are sanctified. - Hebrews 10:1 – 2, 10 - 14

In the old covenant, they kept offering sacrifices because their offering was not eternal, but in the new covenant, the believer is perfected forever, hence redemption is eternal because Jesus is alive, never to die again.

Redemption was not accomplished until Christ was raised from the dead. Redemption is involved in three acts; the death of Jesus, the burial of Jesus, and the bodily resurrection of Jesus. Hence, Jesus had to come out of the dead to show that the price has been paid. Hence, the resurrection of Jesus confirms the work of redemption. The fact that Jesus is alive is the eternal security of our salvation, and the redemption He obtained for us is not temporal but for all time and eternity.

Though he were a Son, yet learned he obedience by the things which he suffered; And being made perfect, he became the author of eternal salvation unto all them that obey him; - Hebrews 5:9

The text of scripture above validates the fact that Jesus offers eternal salvation.

[24] But this man, because he continueth ever, hath an unchangeable priesthood.

[25] Wherefore he is able also to save them to the uttermost that come unto God by him, ***seeing he ever liveth to make intercession for them****.* - Hebrews 7:24 - 25

The scriptural texts above reveal that the basis for Christ's intercession is that He forever sits alive to make intercession; therefore, upon a man believing the gospel, the responsibility for his salvation is that of the saviour; and as seen in the text above, the savior is able to save to the uttermost; that is, completely and forever because He lives forever. Therefore, salvation, redemption, and all of the blessings of God in Christ are eternal.

Salvation is a function of the grace of God, it cannot be merited because it is received freely by faith in the gospel. Everyone who believes is saved, and nobody is more saved than the other because it is the same eternal price that has changed every believer's status and identity forever. Hence, who the believer is today is eternal because the price paid for the believer is eternal.

The fact that Jesus is alive guarantees the believer's salvation completely, as Jesus is the One who keeps the believer eternally.

[23] And the very God of peace sanctify you wholly; and I pray God your whole spirit and soul and body be preserved blameless unto the coming of our Lord Jesus Christ.

[24] Faithful is he that calleth you, who also will do it. - 1Thessalonians 5:23 - 24

[24] Now unto him that is able to keep you from falling, and to present you faultless before the presence of his glory with exceeding joy,

[25] To the only wise God our Saviour, be glory and majesty, dominion and power, both now and ever. Amen. - Jude 1:24 - 25

The Believer is Justified and Made Righteous

Therefore by the deeds of the law there shall no flesh be justified in his sight: for by the law is the knowledge of sin. - Romans3:20

Being justified freely by his grace through the redemption that is in

Christ Jesus: - Romans3:24

The word "justified" here implies a judicial approval; that is to present a ground for the judge to say you are not guilty.

The text of scriptures above reveals that a man cannot be justified by the works of the law in the sight of God. Morality can earn a man justification before men, but not before God. Justification is taught as a work of grace in the epistles; it is free, and it places no demands on man.

To declare, I say, at this time his righteousness: that he might be just, and the justifier of him which believeth in Jesus. - Romans 3:26

Seeing it is one God, which shall justify the circumcision by faith, and uncircumcision through faith. - Romans 3:30

God does not justify works, He justifies those who believe in him, it is in His character that man be justified by faith.

[1] What shall we say then that Abraham our father, as pertaining to the flesh, hath found?

[2] For if Abraham were justified by works, he hath whereof to glory; but not before God.

[3] For what saith the scripture? Abraham believed God, and it was counted unto him for righteousness.

[4 to him that worketh is the reward not reckoned of grace, but of debt.

[5] But to him that worketh not, but believeth on him that justifieth the ungodly, his faith is counted for righteousness. - Romans 4:1 - 5

Abraham was justified by God. God pronounced him righteous

on account of his faith in the gospel.

[8] And the scripture, foreseeing that God would justify the heathen through faith, preached before the gospel unto Abraham, saying, in thee shall all nations be blessed.

[9] So then they which be of faith are blessed with faithful Abraham.

[11] But that no man is justified by the law in the sight of God, it is evident: for, the just shall live by faith. - Galatians 3:8 – 9, 11

Abraham had the gospel preached to him in a promissory note, what gospel?

The gospel that God will bless the nations of the earth in his seed (Christ).

And in thy seed shall all the nations of the earth be blessed; because thou hast obeyed my voice. - Gen 22:18

God blessing every nation in Abraham's seed is what Paul referred to as God justifying the heathen through faith in Christ (the seed), hence Abraham believed this gospel and was blessed. The blessing in this context would mean he was justified, he was called righteous. Hence Gal 3:9 stated emphatically that the same thing will happen to everyone that believe in the gospel like Abraham, such people will be blessed alike, so the just (righteous man) will therefore come into existence by faith alone.

[25] Whom God hath set forth to be a propitiation through faith in his blood, to declare his righteousness for the remission of sins that are past, through the forbearance of God;

[26] To declare, I say, at this time his righteousness: that he might be just, and the justifier of him which believeth in Jesus.- Romans 3:25

- 26

[24] But for us also, to whom it shall be imputed, if we believe on him that raised up Jesus our Lord from the dead;

[25] Who was delivered for our offences, and was raised again for our justification. - Romans 4:24 - 25

The believer is justified by his faith in Christ, and declared righteous. This justification is imputed on the believer by God himself and Christ's resurrection guarantees our justification.

Also the believer has been made righteous in Christ Jesus.

[17] Therefore if any man be in Christ, he is a new creature: old things are passed away; behold, all things are become new.

[18] And all things are of God, who hath reconciled us to himself by Jesus Christ, and hath given to us the ministry of reconciliation;

[19] To wit, that God was in Christ, reconciling the world unto himself, not imputing their trespasses unto them; and hath committed unto us the word of reconciliation.

[20] Now then we are ambassadors for Christ, as though God did beseech you by us: we pray you in Christ's stead, be ye reconciled to God.

[21] For he hath made him to be sin for us, who knew no sin; that we might be made the righteousness of God in him. - 2 Corinthians 5:17 - 21

The word "righteousness" implies that which is just, acceptable, blameless, faultless, proper, moral. It is to stand before God without blame, guilt or condemnation.

[17] For if by one man's offence death reigned by one; much more they which receive abundance of grace and of the gift of righteousness shall reign in life by one, Jesus Christ.)

[18] Therefore as by the offence of one judgment came upon all men

to condemnation; even so by the righteousness of one the free gift came upon all men unto justification of life.

[19] For as by one man's disobedience many were made sinners, so by the obedience of one shall many be made righteous. - Romans 5:17 - 19

Righteousness is a gift. We were made righteous by the obedience of Jesus. The believer's righteousness does not increase or decrease; it is the same from the day he got saved. It is a gift. Hence, the believer does not become more or less righteous. What only increases is his righteousness consciousness, which is by knowledge, which is the acknowledgment of what the word says you are and have. Righteousness is the state of the man in Christ forever.

Even the righteousness of God which is by faith of Jesus Christ unto all and upon all them that believe: for there is no difference: - Romans 3:22

The righteousness of God is that which is obtained by the faithfulness of Christ, for all who believe in His redemptive sacrifice.

But of him are ye in Christ Jesus, who of God is made unto us wisdom, and righteousness, and sanctification, and redemption: - 1 Corinthians 1:30

The believers' righteousness is the righteousness of Jesus and it is a gift received in Christ. Hence, by faith in the gospel, the believer is justified and made righteous eternally.

The Believer is Sanctified and Made Holy

[3] Blessed be the God and Father of our Lord Jesus Christ, who hath blessed us with all spiritual blessings in heavenly places in Christ:

[4] According as he hath chosen us in him before the foundation of the world, that we should be holy and without blame before him in love: - Ephesians 1:3 - 4

Apostle Paul made it clear that the believer has been made holy as one of the blessedness of his identification with Christ. To be holy implies being sacred, separated, and being treated as special. It is similar to the usage of the word "sanctified". By faith in Christ, the believer is separated as special; the believer is sanctified on the basis of what Christ has done.

Unto the church of God which is at Corinth, to them that are sanctified in Christ Jesus, called to be saints, with all that in every place call upon the name of Jesus Christ our Lord, both theirs and ours: - 1 Corinthians 1:2

“To call upon the name Jesus Christ” here implies faith in the offering of Christ for salvation. Therefore, everyone who has believed in Christ is sanctified, hence, the believer is regarded as a saint because he has been sanctified in Christ Jesus.

And such **were** *some of you: but ye are washed, but ye are sanctified, but ye are justified in the name of the Lord Jesus, and by the Spirit of our God.* - 1 Corinthians 6:11

The word “sanctified” has the same implication with the word "holy", it is a word that implies to set apart, to make holy, to keep holy or to be kept apart. Apostle Paul, in earlier verses, referred to the previous state of the believer and the consequent works he produce.

[9] Know ye not that the unrighteous shall not inherit the kingdom of God? Be not deceived: neither fornicators, nor idolaters, nor adulterers, nor effeminate, nor abusers of themselves with mankind,

[10] Nor thieves, nor covetous, nor drunkards, nor revilers, nor extortioners, shall inherit the kingdom of God. - 1 Corinthians 6:9 - 10

The unregenerated man is unrighteous and consequently produces works of unrighteousness, some of which Paul mentioned in the text above. However, it is worthy of note that the tense "were" was employed in 1 Corinthians 6:11 to further affirm that the believer has a change of identity and status in Christ, hence, his present status in Christ is that he is washed, sanctified, and justified by the Spirit he received in his salvation.

Sanctification is taught in the scriptures as a fact of our salvation in Christ. It comes alongside the salvation experience by the Spirit received in salvation. Recall, sanctification implies to set apart, so the believer, by the Spirit received, is set apart unto God and for God.

In the old covenant, after the setting up of the tabernacle, Moses anointed and sanctified (set apart) all the vessels of the tabernacle for God's use.

And it came to pass on the day that Moses had fully set up the tabernacle and had anointed it, and sanctified it, and all the vessels thereof, and had anointed them and sanctified them; - Number 7:1

[9 thou shalt take the anointing oil, and anoint the tabernacle, and all that is therein, and shall hallow it, and all the vessels thereof : and it shall be holy

[10] And thou shalt anoint the alter of the burnt offering, and all his vessels, and sanctify the alter : and it shall be an altar most holy.

[11] And thou shalt anoint the laver and his foot, and sanctify it.

[12] And thou shalt bring Aaron and his sons unto the door of the tabernacle of the congregation, and wash them with water.

[13] And thou shalt put upon Aaron the holy garments, and anoint him, and sanctify him; that he may minister unto me in the priest's office.

[14] And thou shalt bring his sons, and clothe them with clothe them with coats:

[15] And thou shalt anoint them as thou didst anoint their father, that they may minister unto me in the priest's office: for their anointing shall surely be an everlasting priesthood throughout their generations.

[16]Thus did Moses: according to all that the LORD commanded him, so did he. – Exodus 40:9-16

As God commanded Moses to anoint and sanctify the tabernacle and all the vessels therein as a figure of what God was going to do in the new creation.

At salvation, the new creation man is anointed and sanctified (separated) by the God's Spirit unto God, as God's vessel and for God's use. Apostle peter lends credence to this:

But ye are a chosen generation, a royal priesthood, an holy nation, a peculiar people; that ye should shew forth the praises of him who hath called you out of darkness into his marvellous light: - 1 Peter 2:9

Peter further affirms that the believer is a nation set apart from darkness into light to show forth God's praise. The showing forth of God's praise here refers to ministry. Peter associated the believers' sanctification with ministry, he revealed that the believer is sanctified for ministry, which brings to mind Moses' consecration of the vessels in the tabernacle for God's use. Hence, in the salvation of the new creation man, will be found his appointment and consecration for the work of ministry. It is on this basis that Paul taught that the new creation man has been given the ministry of reconciliation and, thus, the ministry gifts in the local assembly are to train and bring the believer up to a place of maturity to the end that he is effective in the work of ministry.

[17] Therefore if any man be in Christ, he is a new creature: old things are passed away; behold, all things are become new.

[18] And all things are of God, who hath reconciled us to himself by Jesus Christ, and hath given to us the ministry of reconciliation;

[19] Now then we are ambassadors for Christ, as though God did beseech you by us: we pray you in Christ stead, be ye reconciled to God. - 2 Corinthian 5:17-20

[11] And he gave some, apostles; and some, prophets; and some evangelists; and some, pastors and teachers;

[12] For the perfecting of the saints, for the work of the ministry, for the edifying of the body Christ:

- Ephesians 4:11-12

The Believer is Sealed

[13]In whom ye also trusted, after that ye heard the word of truth, the gospel of your salvation: in whom also after that ye believed, ye were sealed with that holy Spirit of promise,
[14] Which is the earnest of our inheritance until the redemption of the purchased possession, unto the praise of his glory. - Ephesians 1:13 - 14

The scriptural texts above reveal that upon hearing and believing the gospel of salvation, a man is sealed with the Holy Spirit of promise. That word “sealed”, in this context, implies security or preservation, it implies a permanent mark of ownership.

The man in Christ is sealed with the Holy Spirit of promise as a proof of his redemption. The believer, at salvation, receives the Holy Spirit in him as a seal; a permanent mark of ownership that he has been purchased or redeemed, hence, the reality of the indwelling of the Spirit is the eternal security of the man in Christ because the Spirit lives in the believer forever.

And I will pray the Father, and he shall give you another Comforter, that he may abide with you for ever; - John 14:16

A man cannot be called "redeemed" if he does not have the Holy Spirit in him. The Spirit in him is the result of his redemption. Just as redemption is a function of Christ's work, the Holy Spirit is given as the gift of Christ and no work is required of the believer to receive the Spirit.

And grieve not the holy Spirit of God, whereby ye are sealed unto the day of redemption. - Ephesians 4:30

The believer is sealed by the Spirit of God unto the day of redemption. Recall that the word “redemption” implies to get back, something you paid for, and we have earlier established that the believer is redeemed. However, the believer still awaits bodily redemption, hence, the day of redemption, in this context, is in reference to the day of resurrection when the believer will be redeemed bodily. (this has been well explained in the previous chapter)

The indwelling of the Spirit is the proof that the body of the believer has been paid for by the blood of Jesus Christ and will be redeemed.

But if the Spirit of him that raised up Jesus from the dead dwell in you, he that raised up Christ from the dead shall also quicken your mortal bodies by his Spirit that dwelleth in you. - Romans 8:11

[21]Now he which stablisheth us with you in Christ, and hath anointed us, is God;
[22] Who hath also sealed us, and given the earnest of the Spirit in our hearts. - 2 Corinthians 1:21 - 22

This means that the Spirit in the believer is the assurance that the outward man, the body, will be changed by the Spirit in us.

The Believer is a Citizen of Heaven

Now therefore ye are no more strangers and foreigners, but fellowcitizens with the saints, and of the household of God; - Ephesians 2:19

When a man believes the gospel, he becomes a fellow citizen of the family of God. The word "fellow citizen" refers to the inhabitant of a place; nations, estate of men, hence, by faith in Christ, a man becomes an inhabitant of heaven, that is, God's kingdom, God's nation, God's family.

[22] But ye are come unto mount Sion, and unto the city of the living God, the heavenly Jerusalem, and to an innumerable company of angels,
[23] To the general assembly and church of the firstborn, which are

written in heaven, and to God the Judge of all, and to the spirits of just men made perfect, - Hebrews 12:22 – 23

The believer has come to the city of the living God, the heavenly Jerusalem. The word "come" here is once and for all, it is an action of faith, a present continuous status, that is, the man in Zion (the city of the living God) has come once, and is there forever. Faith in the gospel makes the believer a citizen and it is not possible to be "decitizened", once a citizen is always a citizen because this is predicated upon Jesus offering of His life.

For our conversation is in heaven; from whence also we look for the Saviour, the Lord Jesus Christ: - Philippians 3:20

The words "our conversation" here, implies our citizenship, our commonwealth. As believers, our citizenship is in heaven, hence the believer is not a stranger or foreigner, he's not alien to the commonwealth of heaven. A believer is a member of God's family, he has the same heritage with God.

For this cause I bow my knees unto the Father of our Lord Jesus Christ, - Ephesians 3:14

The family of God is found in Christ, hence, the believer is fathered by God. Being born again is not a mere confession or a change of behavior, it is to be born by the Spirit of God into His household.

As we have therefore opportunity, let us do good unto all men, especially unto them who are of the household of faith. - Galatians 6:10

The word "household" above, implies a domesticated family,

those who live together. This means the common denominator into the household of God is faith in the gospel.

A man who has believed the gospel is born again and he is a member of the household of God. Jesus taught the reality of being born again as being born into the Father's household.

[1] Let not your heart be troubled: ye believe in God, believe also in me.
[2] In my Father's house are many mansions: if it were not so, I would have told you. I go to prepare a place for you. - John 14:1 – 2

The word "house" here implies a household, a family, and the word "mansion" implies a place to dwell, hence, Jesus could not have been referring to physical buildings as the many mansions in his Father's house. A contextual reading will help us understand much better what Jesus meant.

Believest thou not that I am in the Father, and the Father in me? The words that I speak unto you I speak not of myself: but the Father that dwelleth in me, he doeth the works. - John 14:10

Jesus here revealed His union with the Father, that is the Father dwells in Jesus and the Father's house is in Jesus, hence to come to the Father's dwelling place will only be through Jesus.

Jesus saith unto him, I am the way, the truth, and the life: no man cometh unto the Father, but by me. - John 14:6

Therefore, a man that has come to God through Jesus (faith in the gospel) is in the Father's house.

Jesus answered and said unto him, If a man love me, he will keep my words: and my Father will love him, and we will come unto him, and make our abode with him. - John 14:23

Having seen this, John 14:2a can therefore be understood as: "... in my Father's household (family), there are many mansions (many dwelling places)", hence John 14:3:

And if I go and prepare a place for you, I will come again, and receive you unto myself; that where I am, there ye may be also. - John 14:3

Recall as explained in the earlier chapter of this book that Jesus in His incarnation was the only begotten and upon His resurrection, He became the first begotten, which imply Jesus until His resurrection was the only abode of the Father, hence his going to prepare a place for us is to the intent that where he is, we might be also and this He has done by His sacrifice, hence Jesus going to the Father was to make us fit to dwell in the Father's house by His death, burial and resurrection and anyone who has believed in this sacrifice of Jesus today is in the Father's house (family), he has become a member of the Father's family, a citizen of God's heaven, nation, he has come to the city of God, hence, the believer today is a citizen of heaven, he is a family with God, this is the reality of our identification with Christ, all of these are our reality in Christ today as a result of what He has done and our faith in the same.

Having seen all of these realities with overwhelming evidences through scriptures, the believers' identity in Christ which constantly assures him of his salvation, the believer should therefore have just one inference or conclusion of his salvation, his assurance of salvation is validated in the plethora of scriptural evidences which is available to him.

This will lead us to examining the concept of spiritual growth for believers, **how do I grow as a believer?**

CHAPTER THREE

GROWING UP AS A BELIEVER

But grow in grace, and in the knowledge of our Lord and Saviour Jesus Christ. To him be glory both now and for ever - 2 Peter 3:18

It is very important to note that Peter, in the text above, pointed our attention to the fact that to grow in grace is to grow in the knowledge of our Lord and savior Jesus Christ. Therefore, it will be safe to say spiritual growth is primarily knowledge based.

I pray that the sharing of your faith may become effective and powerful because of your accurate knowledge of every good thing which is ours in Christ - Philemon 1:6 (AMP)

Paul here teaches that the believer will have an effective Christian living to the extent to which he grasp and appreciate in his mind the realities of his identity in Christ. Having been born again, having received the indwelling of the Spirit, which is our identification with Christ, the only way we can have an effective Christian living is by a precise appreciation of what we have in Christ.

Not being able to distinguish between salvation and spiritual growth has caused much struggle and inability for many in their Christian walk. However, salvation has been well explained in the earlier chapters of this book as a function of the grace of God; it is only by faith in the gospel of Christ. Hence, salvation is God's responsibility while spiritual growth will be man's responsibility, which is the next step after salvation.

Who will have all men to be saved, and to come unto the knowledge of the truth. - 1 Timothy 2:4

God's desire for all men is to have them saved and come to the knowledge of the truth. This means that salvation is not the end in itself; beyond salvation, it is God's desire that we grow in His knowledge, and this, by extension, will make a man enjoy all the benefits embedded in his salvation.

Salvation is different from spiritual growth. While salvation is solely God's responsibility, spiritual growth is man's responsibility and God's responsibility "in that spiritual growth" however is that while the man is growing he will not die or perish, not being able to draw the line between this will keep the believer double minded and unstable in his mind.

And be not conformed to this world: but be ye transformed by the renewing of your mind, that ye may prove what is that good, and acceptable, and perfect, will of God. - Romans 12:2

The believer is not to be fashioned after this world, rather, he is to be transformed or grow by the renewing of his mind so that he can recognize the will of God. This growth, or transformation, will be done by the Word.

As newborn babes, desire the sincere milk of the word, that ye may grow thereby: - 1 Peter 2:2

Peter here taught that the word of God is the believers' recipe for spiritual growth, hence, he is to have a right attitude to learning if he must grow spiritually.

[18] Oh is own will begat he us with the word of truth, that we should be a kind of firstfruits of his creatures.

[21] Wherefore lay apart all filthiness and superfluity of naughtiness, and receive with meekness the engrafted word, which is able to save your souls.

[222] But be ye doers of the word, and not hearers only, deceiving your own selves

[23]] For if any be a hearer of the word and not a doer, he is like unto a man beholding his natural face in a glass:

[24] For he beholdeth himself, and goeth his way, and straightway forgetteth what manner of man he was

[25] But whoso looketh into the perfect law of liberty, and continueth therein, he being not a forgetful hearer but a doer of the work, this man shall be blessed in his deed - James 1:18,21 - 25

James taughts that the believer having being begotten of God by the word (James 1:18), he therefore shares the same life as the Word, his reality can only be found in the word, hence, for a believer to now hear the Word and not make a practice of it, is for him to live in deception. Hence, James stated that "he is deceiving himself" (James 1:22). This explains why James placed emphasis on the believer being a "doer of the Word and not hearer only". James lets us see that the believer has to be a hearer of the Word to be a doer of the same, hence if a believer hears the Word and does not make a practice of it, he is simply not giving attention to the Word, hence James calls him a forgetful hearer (James 1:24).

However, to be a doer of the Word is to continue to put attention on the Word of God, so James acknowledged that there are believers who will do the Word and believers who will not do the Word, however, they are believers, the difference is that one keeps the knowledge of what he sees while the other forgets, making us see again that spiritual growth is a function of knowledge while by extension reflects in the believer's conduct because a man's action is a reflection of his state of mind (Luke 6:45, Proverbs 4:23).

Hence, Paul in his epistles prays for the believers concerning the knowledge of the Word.

That the God of our Lord Jesus Christ, the Father of glory, may give unto you the spirit of wisdom and revelation in the knowledge of him:

The eyes of your understanding being enlightened; that ye may know what is the hope of his calling, and what the riches of the glory of his inheritance in the saints,

And what is the exceeding greatness of his power to us-ward who believe, according to the working of his mighty power,

Which he wrought in Christ, when he raised him from the dead, and set him at his own right hand in the heavenly places,

Far above all principality, and power, and might, and dominion, and every name that is named, not only in this world, but also in that which is to come: - Ephesians 1:17 – 21

Paul prays that they will know accurately and precisely what God did in Christ and that they will know the power at work towards and in the believer (Colossians 1:9 – 11, Philippians 1:9 – 11, Ephesians 3:14 – 20, Philemon 4 – 6).

All of Paul's prayers focuses on the believer knowing who he is in

Christ, what he has in Christ and what he can do through Christ.

For we are his workmanship, created in Christ Jesus unto good works, which God hath before ordained that we should walk in them. - Ephesians 2:10

The believer is God's handwork, created in Christ Jesus with good works so they can walk in them. Hence, the Christian life is such that it is first received and then lived by the consciousness of the work of God in us.

A man is firstly saved by faith in Christ alone, then he starts to discover what he has received, focusing on God's work in his life, and then he is able to conduct himself in that life, hence the need for him to renew his mind.

For if any be a hearer of the word, and not a doer, he is like unto a man beholding his natural face in a glass: - James 1:23

James, here, refers to the Word as a glass; a mirror, that is, the Word reflects who the believer is to him, hence he used the phrase "beholding his natural face as in a glass", which implies beholding in a mirror the way you were born. That is, the face of birth explains the believer's seeing in the mirror (the word), the reality of who he is in Christ. Hence, the believer is not trying to become who he is already, but rather when he is not practicing the Word which he hears, which is his actual reality in Christ, he is deceiving himself and living in a lie. When James says, "Be ye doers of the Word," he simply means "walk in the reality of who you are," which he says a believer will do effortlessly as he continues to behold the mirror, his realities in Christ. Thus, the degree to which the believer understands what Christ has done for him, is doing in him, and through him, is the degree to which he will have an effective Christian living.

[12] Wherefore, my beloved, as ye have always obeyed, not as in my presence only, but now much more in my absence, ***work out your salvation*** *with fear and trembling*

[13] For it is God which worketh in you both to will and to do of his good pleasure. - Philippians 2:12 – 13

Paul here teaches that believers should work out their salvation. Take note of the phrase "work out," not "work for," because salvation is solely God's work. No man can work for salvation. Paul further explains how the working out will be in verse 13. He says it is by God who is at work in the believer, hence the Christian life is first received and then lived by the consciousness of God's work in us. There is virtually nothing we are able to do with respect to working out our salvation. We are simply to yield ourselves to the workings of the Spirit of God in us. Hence, not doing the word will be tantamount to not living in our reality as believers, because it is God who is at work in the believers.

Now unto him that is able to do exceeding abundantly above all that we ask or think, ***according to the power that worketh in us,*** - Ephesians 3:20

A new heart also will I give you, and a new spirit will I put within you: and I will take away the stony heart out of your flesh, and I will give you an heart of flesh.

And I will put my Spirit within you, and cause you to walk in my statutes, and ye shall keep my judgemnts, and do them - Ezekiel 36:26-27

Ezekiel prophesied about this workings of God in man; His Spirit in man which will cause the man to walk in God's statute.

We have earlier established that when a man believes the gospel, he receives the Spirit.

In whom ye also trusted, after that ye heard the word of truth, the gospel of your salvation: in whom also after that ye believed, ye were sealed with that holy Spirit of promise, - Ephesians 1:13

The believer is sealed with the Spirit in the new birth, and as such he is alive in the Spirit and can walk in the Spirit.
[22] But the fruit of the Spirit is love, joy, peace, longsuffering, gentleness, goodness, faith,
[23] temperance: against such there is no law.
[24] And they that are Christ's have crucified the flesh with the affections and lusts.
[25] If we live in the Spirit, let us also walk in the Spirit. - Galatians 5:22 – 25

Paul was not giving a set of rules or instructions to carry out, but rather he was showing them who they were in Christ. The fruit of the Spirit here in verses 22–23 refers to the believers' "nature" or the result of the Spirit in them. Hence, the nature of the believer is love, joy, peace, longsuffering, etc. Hence, Paul in verse 25 says, since the believer is alive in the Spirit, he should therefore walk in the Spirit, which is to walk in his realities. It is like saying, since you are in the Spirit, continue in the Spirit. It is to conduct oneself in the Spirit. That is to simply live out who we are.

[1] And you hath he quickened, who were dead in trespasses and sins;
[2] Wherein in time past ye walked according to the course of this

world, according to the prince of the power of the air, the spirit that now worketh in the children of disobedience:
[3] Among whom also we all had our conversation in times past in the lusts of our flesh, fulfilling the desires of the flesh and of the mind; and were by nature the children of wrath, even as others. - Ephesians 2:1 – 3

This I say therefore, and testify in the Lord, that ye henceforth walk not as other Gentiles walk, in the vanity of their mind, - Ephesians 4:17

Apostle Paul in the scriptural texts above reveals that the primary place where a walk needs to be done is in the mind of the believer; that is, in the thinking process of a man born again and not in his actions. Hence, the believer has to review his mind and this further reveals that spiritual growth is primarily knowledge-based.

Having seen the place of the mind where growing up spiritually is concerned, it is important to see and note that growing up spiritually is the believer's responsibility and not God's. Thus, the believer is to give due diligence to having his mind renewed, to staying committed and dedicated to his spiritual growth, and this will affect his choice of local church as well.

CHAPTER FOUR

SPIRITUAL GROWTH AND THE LOCAL CHURCH

And I say also unto thee, that thou art Peter, and upon this rock I will build my church; and the gates of hell shall not prevail against it. - Matthew 16:18

The word "church" means the called out, it implies a calling out to come together. When Jesus used the phrase "I will build my church", He qualified the church as His own and what He was to do Himself and He established His church upon His resurrection from the dead.

[14] Blotting out the handwriting of ordinances that was against us, which was contrary to us, and took it out of the way, nailing it to his cross;
[15] And having spoiled principalities and powers, he made a shew of them openly, triumphing over them in it. - Colossians 2:14 – 15

[16] Cease not to give thanks for you, making mention of you in my prayers;
[17] That the God of our Lord Jesus Christ, the Father of glory, may give unto you the spirit of wisdom and revelation in the knowledge of him:
[18] The eyes of your understanding being enlightened; that ye may know what is the hope of his calling, and what the riches of the glory of his inheritance in the saints,

[19] And what is the exceeding greatness of his power to us-ward who believe, according to the working of his mighty power,
[20] Which he wrought in Christ, when he raised him from the dead, and set him at his own right hand in the heavenly places,
[21] Far above all principality, and power, and might, and dominion, and every name that is named, not only in this world, but also in that which is to come:
And hath put all things under his feet, and gave him to be the head over all things to the church,
[22] Which is his body, the fulness of him that filleth all in all. - Ephesians 1:16 – 23

As Jesus rose from the dead, the victory was His church, He rose with His church, hence the church are those He has raised from the dead by identification in His resurrection, hence, every man who has believed the gospel today is identified with Him in His death and resurrection and thus are members of His church.

Therefore, the church is defined in Christ, the church is Christ's called out ones.

But ye are a chosen generation, a royal priesthood, an holy nation, a peculiar people; that ye should shew forth the praises of him who hath called you out of darkness into his marvellous light: - 1 Peter 2:9

[12] Giving thanks unto the Father, which hath made us meet to be partakers of the inheritance of the saints in light:

[13] Who hath delivered us from the power of darkness, and hath translated us into the kingdom of his dear Son. - Colossians 1:12-13

The church is called the body of Christ. Hence, it is a spiritual entity or family whose head (leadership or lordship) is Jesus.

Which he wrought in Christ, when he raised him from the dead, and set him at his own right hand in the heavenly places, - Ephesians 1:20

There is one body, and one Spirit, even as ye are called in one hope of your calling; - Ephesians 4:4

The church of Christ is one family and God is the Father in this family.

Now therefore ye are no more strangers and foreigners, but fellowcitizens with the saints, and of the household of God; - Ephesians 2:19

For ye are all the children of God by faith in Christ Jesus. – Galatians 3:26

LOCAL CHURCH

Having seen that Jesus is the head of His church (His body) and that believers are identified into His body by faith, it is important for us to see another vital aspect of what is called the church.

If therefore the whole church be come together into one place, and all speak with tongues, and there come in those that are unlearned, or unbelievers, will they not say that ye are mad? - 1 Corinthians 14:23

Paul here used church to refer to a gathering of specific people (believers) in a location (in Corinth precisely).

For this cause have I sent unto you Timotheus, who is my beloved son, and faithful in the Lord, who shall bring you into remembrance of my ways which be in Christ, as I teach every where in every church. - 1 Corinthians 4:17

Paul again made it clear that he had taught in several churches, referring to several gatherings of believers in different locations.

So the church was used for a spiritual entity and also for the gathering of believers. Therefore, the local church will refer to a gathering of believers in a particular location. The local church is a part of the universal church—the body of Christ, which consists of believers in every part of the world. The local church is to mirror and reflect the entity of the body of Christ.

But if I tarry long, that thou mayest know how thou oughtest to behave thyself in the house of God, which is the church of the living God, the pillar and ground of the truth. - 1 Timothy 3:15

Paul called it the ground, and pillar of truth. Thus, the gathering of the believer is that atmosphere where the truth of God's Word is taught, received, applied and passed from a generation to another.

After salvation, the next thing a man needs is not the Holy Spirit or power, etc. He already received the Spirit, power when he believed.

But ye are not in the flesh, but in the Spirit, if so be that the Spirit of God dwell in you. Now if any man have not the Spirit of Christ, he is none of his. - Romans 8:9

In whom ye also trusted, after that ye heard the word of truth, the gospel of your salvation: in whom also after that ye believed, ye were sealed with that holy Spirit of promise, - Ephesians 1:13

The next step after salvation is spiritual growth, and this will happen by the believer being introduced to the company of believers, which is a local church.

The believer is born into the family of God—the church. He is not born to abide alone, hence he is to be identified with a local church (company of believers). Just like in the natural, you are not born into a street but into a family, the same way it is when you come to Christ.

When Paul got saved, he was introduced to the company of believers.
[17] And Ananias went his way, and entered into the house; and putting his hands on him said, Brother Saul, the Lord, even Jesus, that appeared unto thee in the way as thou camest, hath sent me, that thou mightest receive thy sight, and be filled with the Holy Ghost.
[18] And immediately there fell from his eyes as it had been scales: and he received sight forthwith, and arose, and was baptized.
[19] And when he had received meat, he was strengthened. Then was Saul certain days with the disciples which were at Damascus. – Acts 9:17 – 19

No one grows in isolation, spiritual growth happens in the company of believers, hence, the next thing a man needs after salvation is to identify with a local church, he must find a place where he can grow spiritually.

FINDING A LOCAL CHURCH

After salvation, the most important choice a man will make is his choice of a local church. Your company of believers says a lot about your spirituality, and the local church is to help the believer grow spiritually. Hence, finding or choosing a local church should be prayerfully and purposefully done. A believer should not just be concerned about the proximity of the church location to his house or get carried away by good music, first-timer gifts, drama, good ambience, etc. or choose a particular local church because it is your friends' church or family church or you will have connections there. All these considerations are carnal and have no benefit spiritually. Hence, before choosing a local church, it is important to ask some questions to be certain if the local church is suitable for your spiritual growth:

Is the Word of God given first place there?

But if I tarry long, that thou mayest know how thou oughtest to behave thyself in the house of God, which is the church of the living God, the pillar and ground of the truth. - 1 Timothy 3:15

The local church should be a place where the truth of God's Word is taught, received, applied, and passed from generation to generation. The early church was given to the teaching of God's word, and any local church fulfilling God's purpose today should also be given to the teaching of the Word.

God has set men in the local church to watch over other believers and this they are to do via teaching and instruction.

Remember them which have the rule over you, who have spoken unto you the word of God: whose faith follow, considering the end of their conversation. - Hebrews 13:17

[1] The elders which are among you I exhort, who am also an elder, and a witness of the sufferings of Christ, and also a partaker of the glory that shall be revealed:
[2] Feed the flock of God which is among you, taking the oversight thereof, not by constraint, but willingly; not for filthy lucre, but of a ready mind; – 1 Peter 5:1 – 2

They are to labour in word, and in doctrine.

Let the elders that rule well be counted worthy of double honour, especially they who labour in the word and doctrine. - 1 Timothy 5:17

They are to present you perfect, and mature in Christ.

Whom we preach, warning every man, and teaching every man in all wisdom; that we may present every man perfect in Christ Jesus: - Colossians 1:28

[11] And he gave some, apostles; and some, prophets; and some, evangelists; and some, pastors and teachers;
[12] For the perfecting of the saints, for the work of the ministry, for the edifying of the body of Christ:
[13] Till we all come in the unity of the faith, and of the knowledge of the Son of God, unto a perfect man, unto the measure of the stature of the fulness of Christ:
[14] That we henceforth be no more children, tossed to and fro, and carried about with every wind of doctrine, by the sleight of men, and cunning craftiness, whereby they lie in wait to deceive; – Ephesians 4: 11 – 14

If spiritual growth is primarily knowledge based as we have earlier seen, then the place of teaching meetings in the local church cannot be understated. Teaching meetings were prominent in the early church. Paul taught the disciples in Traos from evening till morning.

[7] And upon the first day of the week, when the disciples came together to break bread, Paul preached unto them, ready to depart on the morrow; and continued his speech until midnight.
[8] And there were many lights in the upper chamber, where they were gathered together.
[9] And there sat in a window a certain young man named Eutychus, being fallen into a deep sleep: and as Paul was long preaching, he sunk down with sleep, and fell down from the third loft, and was taken up dead.
[10] And Paul went down, and fell on him, and embracing him said, Trouble not yourselves; for his life is in him.
[11] When he therefore was come up again, and had broken bread, and eaten, and talked a long while, even till break of day, so he departed. - Acts 20:7 – 11

Paul testified that he declared to the church at Ephesus all the counsel of God.

[20] And how I kept back nothing that was profitable unto you, but have shewed you, and have taught you publickly, and from house to house,

[27] For I have not shunned to declare unto you all the counsel of God.

[30] Also of your own selves shall men arise, speaking perverse things, to draw away disciples after them. - Acts 20:20, 27, 30

Jesus, after He rose from the dead, spent His days teaching His disciples.

[2] Until the day in which he was taken up, after that he through the Holy Ghost had given commandments unto the apostles whom he had chosen:
[3] To whom also he shewed himself alive after his passion by many infallible proofs, being seen of them forty days, and speaking of the things pertaining to the kingdom of God: - Acts 1:2 – 3

After 3000 souls were added to the church on the day of Pentecost, they continued in the apostles' doctrine (teaching, explanation).

The early apostles appointed men over natural responsibilities so they could focus on the ministry of the Word, and prayer in the local church.

[3] Wherefore, brethren, look ye out among you seven men of honest report, full of the Holy Ghost and wisdom, whom we may appoint over this business.
[4] But we will give ourselves continually to prayer, and to the ministry of the word. - Acts 6:3 – 4

It appears that the teaching ministry was a core activity in the early church. The Word of God was given first place. Hence, this should be a major factor in considering your choice of local assembly. It is also very vitally important to note that the teachings in the local church must find its root in the Holy Scriptures. It must be according to the teachings of the early apostles. Any deviation from that will be false doctrine/ teachings.

[15] And that from a child thou hast known the holy scriptures, which are able to make thee wise unto salvation through faith which is in Christ Jesus.

[16] All scripture is given by inspiration of God, and is profitable for doctrine, for reproof, for correction, for instruction in righteousness:

[17] That the man of God may be perfect, throughly furnished unto all good works. - 2 Timothy 3:15 – 17

Only the scriptures are valid for teaching and evidence. The scriptures remain the basis for our evidences not experiences, hearsay, human opinion or cultural beliefs hence, the local church must be found submitted to the authority of the scriptures.

Is the local church committed to prayer?

But we will give ourselves continually to prayer, and to the ministry of the word. – Acts 6:4

The early apostles took seriously the ministry of prayer, hence, they handed over natural responsibilities so that they could keenly attend to the ministry of prayer.

The first time the church of Jesus gathered to wait for the outpouring of the Holy Ghost, they were in prayer and supplication.

These all continued with one accord in prayer and supplication, with the women, and Mary the mother of Jesus, and with his brethren. - Acts 1:14

On the day of Pentecost, after 3000 souls were added to the church, it is recorded that they continued in prayers.

And they continued stedfastly in the apostles' doctrine and fellowship, and in breaking of bread, and in prayers. - Acts 2:42

The act of the church continuing in prayers shows that the church was diligent in prayer and had a consistent lifestyle of prayer, even in the face of persecution, their first reaction is prayer and not protest.

[23] And being let go, they went to their own company, and reported all that the chief priests and elders had said unto them.
[24] And when they heard that, they lifted up their voice to God with one accord, and said, Lord, thou art God, which hast made heaven, and earth, and the sea, and all that in them is: Acts 4:23 , 24

Observe the apostles had just been back and warned not to preach in Jesus name, yet their first reaction was to go back to their company (the local church) to pray and as they prayed, they got more bold to preach and had more people saved.

Also, when Peter was captured to be killed, the church prayed for his deliverance.

Peter therefore was kept in prison: but prayer was made without ceasing of the church unto God for him. - Acts 12:5

The early church had a lifestyle and culture of prayer. The early apostles understood the possibilities of prayer, they knew prayer makes power available and they were devoted to the ministry of prayer, more reason why they were able to turn their world upside. Even in the midst of persecution, the church prevailed.

The early church had a lifestyle and a culture of prayer. The early apostles understood the possibilities of prayer. They knew prayer makes power available and they were devoted to the ministry of prayer. This is another reason why they were able to turn their world upside down. Even in the midst of persecution, the church prevailed.

A church that is not given to prayer consistently is a church that does not trust the power of God at work in the church. It is a church that trusts and depends on human strength rather than God. Hence, such gatherings will be given to natural gimmicks to promote growth amid other aspirations, because prayer is a demonstration of our trust and dependence on God. In our Lord and Savior's earthly walk and ministry, He was given to the ministry of prayer.

And when he had sent the multitudes away, he went up into a mountain apart to pray: and when the evening was come, he was there alone. - Matthew 14:23

And he withdrew himself into the wilderness, and prayed. - Luke 5:16

Jesus went apart to pray.

And it came to pass in those days, that he went out into a mountain to pray, and continued all night in prayer to God. - Luke 6:12

Jesus prayed all night.

Then cometh Jesus with them unto a place called Gethsemane, and saith unto the disciples, Sit ye here, while I go and pray yonder. - Matthew 26:36

Jesus took his disciples to pray.

Hence, if the believers are disciples/followers of Jesus today then we must also be found given to prayer. Jesus in His earthly walk left for us examples to follow which one of them is a lifestyle of prayer.

For even hereunto were ye called: because Christ also suffered for us, leaving us an example, that ye should follow his steps: - 1 Peter 2:21

If Jesus, the head and lord of the church, was given to prayer then the church also should be given to the same.
Prayer is the bedrock of success in life and ministry. When we pray, we make power available to change life situations and circumstances. If we must see God's divine hand in all our affairs in life and ministry then we must be found given to prayer individually and also as a local church.

There are plethora of instructions in scriptures for believers to pray.

Be careful for nothing; but in every thing by prayer and supplication with thanksgiving let your requests be made known unto God. - Philippians 4:6

Here Paul is saying we should make our request known to God which implies making our desires known to God hence prayer cannot be by thinking, words have to be spoken. It is the believer making a request of what he desires before a higher authority.

Is the local church committed to evangelism and discipleship?
Evangelism is an act of reaching out to the lost/unsaved, while

discipleship implies making students of the gospel – those who have been saved.

Who will have all men to be saved, and to come unto the knowledge of the truth. - 1 Timothy 2:4

God's desire is to have all men saved and come to the knowledge of the truth, and he has given this responsibility to the church to carry out. This was the practice of the early church, they were given to reaching out to the lost and discipling them. Peter on the day of Pentecost preached the gospel and 3000 people were saved, and they continued in the apostle's doctrine and fellowship.

[38] Then Peter said unto them, Repent, and be baptized every one of you in the name of Jesus Christ for the remission of sins, and ye shall receive the gift of the Holy Ghost.

[41] Then they that gladly received his word were baptized: and the same day there were added unto them about three thousand souls.

[42] And they continued stedfastly in the apostles' doctrine and fellowship, and in breaking of bread, and in prayers. - Acts 2:38, 41 – 42

The focus of the local church must, therefore, be to train believers to go out to win souls and disciple them. The ministry of reconciliation is for every believers, upon being saved comes a responsibility to make manifest the savour of Christ's knowledge by preaching the gospel.

[14] For the love of Christ constraineth us; because we thus judge, that if one died for all, then were all dead:

[15] And that he died for all, that they which live should not henceforth live unto themselves, but unto him which died for them, and rose again.

[16] Wherefore henceforth know we no man after the flesh: yea,

though we have known Christ after the flesh, yet now henceforth know we him no more.
[17] Therefore if any man be in Christ, he is a new creature: old things are passed away; behold, all things are become new.
[18] And all things are of God, who hath reconciled us to himself by Jesus Christ, and hath given to us the ministry of reconciliation; - 2 Corinthians 5:14 – 18

Now thanks be unto God, which always causeth us to triumph in Christ, and maketh manifest the savour of his knowledge by us in every place. - 2 Corinthians 2:14

It is the will of God that every believer be actively involved in the ministry of reconciliation, hence, the local church should be devoted to evangelism, and discipleship with a deep sense of purpose, and responsibility as a commission received of Jesus Christ, the head of the church. A good local church will therefore lay emphasis on this and see to it that the membership are so trained to effectively carry out the same.

[11] And he gave some, apostles; and some, prophets; and some, evangelists; and some, pastors and teachers;
[12] For the perfecting of the saints, for the work of the ministry, for the edifying of the body of Christ:
[13] Till we all come in the unity of the faith, and of the knowledge of the Son of God, unto a perfect man, unto the measure of the stature of the fulness of Christ: - Ephesians 4:11 – 13

Evangelist Reinhard Bonnke said “The church that is not going after the lost is lost”, and this is entirely true as the responsibility to reach out to the lost is given to the church. Hence, a local church that's not actively given to evangelism is one that's not walking in the will of God, and so it is for all its membership.

Evangelism is not inviting people to church or sharing tracts for publicity of church meetings. Evangelism is the preaching of the gospel to the unsaved and this is the great commission Christ gave to His church.

And he said unto them, Go ye into all the world, and preach the gospel to every creature. - Mark 16:15

The gospel is the good news about Christ. The fact and charter of the gospel is how Christ died for the sin of the world, was buried, and was raised, the third day, for our justification.

[2] By which also ye are saved, if ye keep in memory what I preached unto you, unless ye have believed in vain.
[3] For I delivered unto you first of all that which I also received, how that Christ died for our sins according to the scriptures; - 1 Corinthians 15:2 – 3

The gospel which is the good news about Christ is, in itself, the power of God to save (Romans 1:16). Hence, a suitable local church will train its membership how to be effective in sharing the gospel with other people.

Does the local church give room for the expression of the gifts of the Spirit?

In the earlier chapter of this book, we have established the fact that the man in Christ receives the indwelling of the Spirit upon believing the gospel. It is not possible to be a child of God and not have the Spirit of God.

But ye are not in the flesh, but in the Spirit, if so be that the Spirit of God dwell in you. Now if any man have not the Spirit of Christ, he is none of his. - Romans 8:9

The Spirit of God in the believer is the Spirit of sonship.

And because ye are sons, God hath sent forth the Spirit of his Son into your hearts, crying, Abba, Father. - Galatians 4:6

The Spirit in the believer is the proof of his redemption.

[13] In whom ye also trusted, after that ye heard the word of truth, the gospel of your salvation: in whom also after that ye believed, ye were sealed with that holy Spirit of promise,

[14] Which is the earnest of our inheritance until the redemption of the purchased possession, unto the praise of his glory. - Ephesians 1:13 – 14

A believer possess the Spirit upon salvation; coming with that Spirit are supernatural abilities or faculties otherwise known as the gifts in the Spirit.

Now there are diversities of gifts, but the same Spirit. - 1 Corinthians 12:4

"Diversities" here implies a singular thing that has various faculties in it; like an orange split into 12 parts, or a phone with several functions. This means we have just one Spirit but in the Spirit we now have diversities, hence, it is in salvation that we received all these gifts of the Spirit. We do not look for them outside salvation. That is why Paul now explains further in 1 Corinthians 12:7:

But the manifestation of the Spirit is given to every man to profit withal.- 1 Corinthians 12:7

The word "manifestation" here implies an unveiling, that is a full disclosure. Hence, Paul implies that every believer has the indwelling of the Spirit. The same Spirit every believer receives at salvation. None has more Spirit than the other. It is the same full disclosure of the Spirit we possess (when something is fully disclosed, it cannot be opened again, hence the manifestation of the Spirit is once and for all, it is the profiting that we now see).

Paul then says "it is given to us to profit withal" which implies it is for the common good of the church, hence, the Spirit of God in the believer is for ministry. Salvation – getting born again, must therefore be seen as a platform for ministry; as a platform to be a blessing.

The Holy Ghost convinces a man about the gospel, makes a him His home, makes him God's son, and also makes him God's minister.

[8] For to one is given by the Spirit the word of wisdom; to another the word of knowledge by the same Spirit;
[9] To another faith by the same Spirit; to another the gifts of healing by the same Spirit;
[10] To another the working of miracles; to another prophecy; to another discerning of spirits; to another divers kinds of tongues; to another the interpretation of tongues: - 1 Corinthians 12:8 – 10

Apostle Paul listed, in the above scriptural text, all the diversities of the gifts in the Spirit, which are the abilities of the Spirit in the believer, and by extension the ability of every believer. Observe the phrases "To one... To another...", they do not refer to persons as though Paul were saying some persons are given word of knowledge, then another is given word of wisdom. No! That will contradict what he had earlier taught that all the diversities are resident in the Spirit in the believer.

Those words "To one... To another..." will refer to the diversities or varieties of the gifts and not a person because it is the same Spirit. The differences cannot be in persons, they can only be in ministry or operation. It is like saying, in the Spirit resident in the believer, there is an ability that reveals past and present circumstances (word of knowledge), another ability in that same Spirit that reveals future events and counsel (word of wisdom), etc.

The list of the diversities of the Spirit by Paul based on their operations can be put into the following classifications:

- **Vocal or utterance gifts** – these are gifts in the spirit of the believer, that have to do with speaking. They are: tongues, interpretations of tongues, and prophecy.
- **Revelation gifts** – these are gifts in the spirit of the believer that reveals, and unveils facts about places, people, events and things. They are: word of wisdom, word of knowledge, and discernment of spirits.
- **Power gifts** – these are gifts in the spirit of the believer that do or accomplish tasks such as "healings" and "miracles". They are: the gift of healings, working of miracles and gift of faith.

All these abilities are resident in the believer, and are within the stewardship of the believer. They cannot be lost because the manifestation of the Spirit can only be once and for all.

How is it then, brethren? when ye come together, every one of you hath a psalm, hath a doctrine, hath a tongue, hath a revelation, hath an interpretation. Let all things be done unto edifying. - 1 Corinthians 14:26

Paul's instruction here reveals that every believer (each one of them) should have a Psalm, doctrine (teaching), a tongue, a revelation, and an interpretation in believer's gathering.

All these are supernatural abilities in the Spirit in the believer, as earlier seen, and Paul's instruction here is for all believers to participate in the gifts, in their spirit, in order to be a blessing to other believers. Technically, Paul made it clear that every believer has this supernatural ability in him and should seek to edify others with it in the local church. Hence, a suitable local church will be one that teaches the believer to be effective in participating in the gifts in the Spirit, and also gives room for the flow of the same so the believers could be a blessing to one another.

This was the pattern of the early church too (Acts 2:4, Acts 4:31, Acts 13:1 – 2, Acts 10:45 – 46, Acts 19:6). Paul later taught and gave instruction to churches with respect to this.

[18] And be not drunk with wine, wherein is excess; but be filled with the Spirit;

[19] Speaking to yourselves in psalms and hymns and spiritual songs, singing and making melody in your heart to the Lord; - Ephesians 5:18 – 19

Let the word of Christ dwell in you richly in all wisdom; teaching and admonishing one another in psalms and hymns and spiritual songs, singing with grace in your hearts to the Lord. - Colossians 3:16

Having seen the critical factors that must be taking into consideration in a believer's choice of local assembly, we will further examine the kind of meetings and activities that should be held by the local church in view of this factors.

The scripture reveals the kind of meetings and activities that should be held in the local church.

Teaching Meetings

The teaching meetings are the primary meeting of the church. It is very important in ensuring the spiritual growth of its members. The teaching meeting is one where the scriptures are taught and explained. It is like a school where students come to learn.

[18] And Jesus came and spake unto them, saying, All power is given unto me in heaven and in earth.
[19] Go ye therefore, and teach all nations, baptizing them in the name of the Father, and of the Son, and of the Holy Ghost:
[20] Teaching them to observe all things whatsoever I have commanded you: and, lo, I am with you always, even unto the end of the world. Amen. - Matthew 28:18 – 20

The way the church is going to make disciples of men is by teaching, and explanation. This teaching will be restricted to the doctrine of Christ.

Jesus spent 40 days explaining the scriptures concerning Himself (Luke 24:25 – 27, 44 – 49; Acts 1:2 – 3).

Paul taught from evening till the next morning, he had a kind of "bible study vigil".

[7] And upon the first day of the week , when the disciples came together to break bread, Paul preached unto them, ready to depart on the morrow; and continued his speech until midnight
[8] And there were many lights in the upper chamber, where they gathered together
[9] And there sat upon. And there sat in a window a certain young man named Eutychus, being fallen into a deep sleep: and as Paul was long preaching, he sunk down with sleep, and fell down from the third loft, and was taken up dead.

[10] And Paul went down, and fell on him, and embracing him said, Trouble not yourselves; for his life is in him.

[11] When he therefore was come up again, and had broken bread, and eaten, and talked a long while, even till break of day, so he departed. - Acts 20:7 - 11

Then called he them in, and lodged them. And on the morrow Peter went away with them, and certain brethren from Joppa accompanied him. - Acts 28:23

The teaching meeting was the prominent meeting of the early church. They had long hours, and moment of explaining scriptures, which further affirms that the church is a bible school where believers come to learn. This defines Christian life.

Paul spoke of how he taught his disciples daily in Ephesus, both publicly and from house to house declaring all the counsel of God.

[20] And how I kept back nothing that was profitable unto you, but have shewed you, and have taught you publickly, and from house to house,

[27] For I have not shunned to declare unto you all the counsel of God - Acts 20:20,27

Also Paul's letter to Timothy and Titus were emphatic on teaching.

And the things that thou hast heard of me among many witnesses, the same commit thou to faithful men, who shall be able to teach others also. - 2 Timothy 2:2

The local church is a place where the believers are taught so they can teach others. A believer in Christ will therefore be doing himself a lot of good by choosing a local church where he will have himself taught, rooted, and grounded in the doctrine of Christ.

Prayer Meetings

This is also a primary meeting in the local church. In the early church, prayer meetings were regularly held alongside the teaching meeting. Both the teaching and prayer meetings carry out the function of the church more than any other Christian meeting.

Basically, the prayer meeting is where we come together to pray and the early church had such meetings.

These all continued with one accord in prayer and supplication, with the women, and Mary the mother of Jesus, and with his brethren. - Acts 1:14

They were holding a prayer meeting before the day of Pentecost.

*And they **continued stedfastly** in the apostles' doctrine and fellowship, and in breaking of bread, and **in prayers**.* - Acts 2:42

After 3000 souls were saved, and added to the church on the day of Pentecost, they were said to continue in prayers.

And being let go, they went to their own company, and reported all that the chief priests and elders had said unto them.
And when they heard that, they lifted up their voice to God with one accord, and said, Lord, thou art God, which hast made heaven, and earth, and the sea, and all that in them is: - Acts 4:23 – 24, 31

Peter therefore was kept in prison: but prayer was made without ceasing of the church unto God for him. - Acts 12:5

It is worthy of note, that even in the face of persecutions; the early church was still given to prayers.

The early apostles, in their epistles leaves for the church instructions about prayer.

Rejoicing in hope; patient in tribulation; ***continuing instant in prayer***; - Romans 12:12

Prayer ought to be a continuing activity of the church.

Praying always with all prayer and supplication in the Spirit, and watching thereunto with all perseverance and supplication for all saints; - Ephesians 6:18

Pray without ceasing. - 1 Thessalonians 5:17

Prayer meetings ought to be a regular meeting in the church such that it should be held often.

In prayer meetings, we pray the following prayers:

[15] Wherefore I also, after I heard of your faith in the Lord Jesus, and love unto all the saints,

[16 not to give thanks for you, making mention of you in my prayers;

[17] That the God of our Lord Jesus Christ, the Father of glory, may give unto you the spirit of wisdom and revelation in the knowledge of him:

[18] The eyes of your understanding being enlightened; that ye may know what is the hope of his calling, and what the riches of the glory of his inheritance in the saints,

[19] And what is the exceeding greatness of his power to us-ward who believe, according to the working of his mighty power, - Ephesians 1:15 – 19

We pray for ourselves and fellow believers to grow in the knowledge of God's Word: Since spiritual growth is growth in the knowledge of our salvation. This was the focus of Paul's prayers for believers (Ephesians 3:14 – 19, Philippians 1:4 – 6, Philippians 1:9 – 11, Colossians 1:9 – 11). Thus, we pray for insight for ourselves and other believers.

We pray for ministers of the gospel.

Praying always with all prayer and supplication in the Spirit, and watching thereunto with all perseverance and supplication for all saints; - Ephesians 6:18

Praying always for all saints will involve the members, and leaders of the church, our ministers (pastors and leaders). Paul often requests that the church pray for him, this technically suggests that ministers of the gospel ought to be prayed for, especially for the work of ministry.

[19] And for me, that utterance may be given unto me, that I may open my mouth boldly, to make known the mystery of the gospel,
[20] For which I am an ambassador in bonds: that therein I may speak boldly, as I ought to speak. - Ephesians 6:19 – 20

Continue in prayer, and watch in the same with thanksgiving;

Withal praying also for us, that God would open unto us a door of utterance, to speak the mystery of Christ, for which I am also in bonds: - Colossians 4:2

We pray for utterance, and boldness to preach and teach the gospel as they ought to.

[30] Now I beseech you, brethren, for the Lord Jesus Christ's sake, and for the love of the Spirit, that ye strive together with me in your prayers to God for me;
[31] That I may be delivered from them that do not believe in Judaea;

and that my service which I have for Jerusalem may be accepted of the saints; - Romans 15:30 – 31

[1] Finally, brethren, pray for us, that the word of the Lord may have free course, and be glorified, even as it is with you:
[2] And that we may be delivered from unreasonable and wicked men: for all men have not faith. - 2 Thessalonians 3:1 – 2

We pray for ministers of the gospel, for their safety and preservation and that their ministry be received without hinderance.

Through mighty signs and wonders, by the power of the Spirit of God; so that from Jerusalem, and round about unto Illyricum, I have fully preached the gospel of Christ. - Romans 15:19

By stretching forth thine hand to heal; and that signs and wonders may be done by the name of thy holy child Jesus. - Acts 4:30

We also pray that signs and wonders are wrought through their ministries.

Prayer meetings are an integral part of the church. They are not special meetings neither are they meetings meant for only the "prayer unit" members of a local church. No! Prayer is the responsibility of every believer.

Evangelistic/Outreach Meetings

These are meetings where we have the unsaved, the lost reached out to, by the preaching of the gospel. They are usually done outside church meetings. They involve going out to the world where the sinners are, to win them over to Christ. This can be in form of one-on-one evangelism, two-by-two evangelism, gospel crusades, prison evangelism, village/rural evangelism and so on. It is done with the sole purpose of getting the lost saved through the preaching of the gospel.

We see examples of such meetings in the book of acts.

[38] Then Peter said unto them, Repent, and be baptized every one of you in the name of Jesus Christ for the remission of sins, and ye shall receive the gift of the Holy Ghost.
[39] For the promise is unto you, and to your children, and to all that are afar off, even as many as the Lord our God shall call.
[49] And with many other words did he testify and exhort, saying, Save yourselves from this untoward generation.
[41] Then they that gladly received his word were baptized: and the same day there were added unto them about three thousand souls. - Acts 2:38 – 41

Peter got 3000 men saved on the day of Pentecost.

In Acts 10:32 – 40, Peter reached out to the house of Cornelius and got all of Cornelius' household saved by the preaching of the gospel.

[1] And it came to pass, that, while Apollos was at Corinth, Paul having passed through the upper coasts came to Ephesus: and finding certain disciples,
[2] He said unto them, Have ye received the Holy Ghost since ye believed? And they said unto him, We have not so much as heard whether there be any Holy Ghost.
[3] And he said unto them, Unto what then were ye baptized? And they said, Unto John's baptism.
[4] Then said Paul, John verily baptized with the baptism of repentance, saying unto the people, that they should believe on him which should come after him, that is, on Christ Jesus.
[5] When they heard this, they were baptized in the name of the Lord Jesus.

[6] And when Paul had laid his hands upon them, the Holy Ghost came on them; and they spake with tongues, and prophesied. - Acts 19:1 – 6

Paul also preached the gospel to certain disciples (of course, not Christ's disciples). They were religious folks in Ephesus. Paul got them saved and filled them with the Holy Ghost. As they heard Paul preach the gospel (verse 4), they believed. That is what Luke recorded as they were baptized in the name of Jesus (verse 5). "To be baptized in the name of the Lord Jesus" implies being immersed into the body of Christ, being engrafted into the family of God by faith in the gospel.

A key characteristic of evangelistic meetings is the working of miracles and healings. Evangelistic meetings give the church a platform and an opportunity to do the supernatural in order to draw the attention of the unsaved to their message.

In evangelistic meetings, the power gifts are usually the most prominent among the gifts of (in) the Spirit. Believers usually have the opportunity to express their gifts by ministering to the needs of the unsaved supernaturally, which often helps grab the attention of the unsaved to listen to the gospel being preached. This pattern was used by Jesus and the early apostles during their earthly walk.

Jesus raised Lazarus from the dead and many of the Jews believed in Him (John 11:21 – 26, 39 – 45).

Peter healed a man who was lame from his mother's womb and used the opportunity to preach the gospel to others (Acts 3:2–13).

The believer/church, today, have the same capacity, and thus commissioned by the Lord Jesus to preach the gospel with signs following.

[15] And he said unto them, Go ye into all the world, and preach the gospel to every creature.
[16] He that believeth and is baptized shall be saved; but he that believeth not shall be damned.
[17] And these signs shall follow them that believe; In my name shall they cast out devils; they shall speak with new tongues;
[18] They shall take up serpents; and if they drink any deadly thing, it shall not hurt them; they shall lay hands on the sick, and they shall recover. - Mark 16:15 – 18

Healing Meetings

These are meetings specially held to minister to the sick. The focus of healing meetings is usually the sick. Many times, healing meetings are part of evangelistic meetings. An example of this will be seen in Acts 13 where Peter and James healed the sick and then preached the gospel.

[6] Then Peter said, Silver and gold have I none; but such as I have give I thee: In the name of Jesus Christ of Nazareth rise up and walk.
[7] And he took him by the right hand, and lifted him up: and immediately his feet and ankle bones received strength.
[8] And he leaping up stood, and walked, and entered with them into the temple, walking, and leaping, and praising God.
[9] And all the people saw him walking and praising God:
[10] And they knew that it was he which sat for alms at the Beautiful gate of the temple: and they were filled with wonder and amazement at that which had happened unto him.

[11] And as the lame man which was healed held Peter and John, all the people ran together unto them in the porch that is called Solomon's, greatly wondering.
[12] And when Peter saw it, he answered unto the people, Ye men of Israel, why marvel ye at this? or why look ye so earnestly on us, as though by our own power or holiness we had made this man to walk?
[13] The God of Abraham, and of Isaac, and of Jacob, the God of our fathers, hath glorified his Son Jesus; whom ye delivered up, and denied him in the presence of Pilate, when he was determined to let him go.- Acts 3:6 - 13

Philip also healed the sick and preached the gospel in Samaria.

[4] Therefore they that were scattered abroad went every where preaching the word.
[5] Then Philip went down to the city of Samaria, and preached Christ unto them.
[6] And the people with one accord gave heed unto those things which Philip spake, hearing and seeing the miracles which he did.
[7] For unclean spirits, crying with loud voice, came out of many that were possessed with them: and many taken with palsies, and that were lame, were healed.
[8] And there was great joy in that city. - Acts 8:4 – 8

The healing ministry is a vital part and parcel of Jesus' ministry, and it is often used as an opportunity to preach the gospel.

[17] And these signs shall follow them that believe; In my name shall they cast out devils; they shall speak with new tongues;
[18] They shall take up serpents; and if they drink any deadly thing, it shall not hurt them; they shall lay hands on the sick, and they shall recover. - Mark 16:17 – 18

[14] And when Jesus was come into Peter's house, he saw his wife's mother laid, and sick of a fever.
[15] And he touched her hand, and the fever left her: and she arose, and ministered unto them.
[16] When the even was come, they brought unto him many that

were possessed with devils: and he cast out the spirits with his word, and healed all that were sick: - Matthew 8:14 – 16

And Jesus went about all the cities and villages, teaching in their synagogues, and preaching the gospel of the kingdom, and healing every sickness and every disease among the people. - Matthew 9:35

The early apostles, also, were given to the healing ministry of Jesus.

[12] And by the hands of the apostles were many signs and wonders wrought among the people; (and they were all with one accord in Solomon's porch.
[13] And of the rest durst no man join himself to them: but the people magnified them.
[14] And believers were the more added to the Lord, multitudes both of men and women.)
[15] Insomuch that they brought forth the sick into the streets, and laid them on beds and couches, that at the least the shadow of Peter passing by might overshadow some of them.
[16] There came also a multitude out of the cities round about unto Jerusalem, bringing sick folks, and them which were vexed with unclean spirits: and they were healed every one. - Acts 5:12 – 16
[11] And God wrought special miracles by the hands of Paul:
[12] So that from his body were brought unto the sick handkerchiefs or aprons, and the diseases departed from them, and the evil spirits went out of them. - Acts 19:11 – 12

Healing was a vital part of Jesus' ministry. Jesus also held healing meetings.

But so much the more went there a fame abroad of him: and great multitudes came together to hear, and to be healed by him of their infirmities. - Luke 5:15

Also, believers can get sick and believe God for healing and be healed, hence, the healing meeting can be, both, to the saved and the unsaved. In Acts 5, both believers and unbelievers were healed.

These are the meetings or activities we would see in the early church, and most prominent are the Teaching and the Prayer meeting hence, a good local church today will follow that same pattern, as this is paramount to the fulfilment of her mission in Christ.

A believer therefore must prayerfully and thoughtfully make his choice of local assembly considering all of these factors as the local church play a critical role in him fulfilling God's plan for his life hence, to be flippant about his choice of local church is to be flippant about his Christian life.

CHAPTER FIVE

SPIRITUAL GROWTH AND THE BELIEVER

We have earlier established from scriptures that salvation is God's role and responsibility. Man's role, where salvation is concerned, is simply to receive the gift of salvation by faith in the gospel.

[8] For by grace are ye saved through faith; and that not of yourselves: it is the gift of God:

[9] Not of works, lest any man should boast.

[10] For we are his workmanship, created in Christ Jesus unto good works, which God hath before ordained that we should walk in them. - Ephesians 2:8-10

The believer is not saved by performance but by grace; by faith in the gospel a man receives eternal salvation.

Therefore He is able to save forever (completely, perfectly, for eternity) those who come to God through Him, since He always lives to intercede and intervene on their behalf (with God) - Hebrew 7:25 (amp)

The above text made it clear that the salvation God offers in Christ is forever. The savior is able to save completely and perfectly, that is, to the end, Jesus forever sits alive at the right hand of God, to make intercessions for the saints, hence, salvation is the savior's responsibility. The believer's salvation is not in his hand but in Christ's hand, hence, the believer has eternal security in Christ.

[28] And I give unto them eternal life; and they shall never perish, neither shall any man pluck them out of my hand.

[29] My Father, which gave them me, is greater than all; and no man is able to pluck them out of my Father's hand. - John 10:28-29

The believer has passed from death to life and cannot come into condemnation because he has eternal life in Christ Jesus.

[24] Verily, verily, I say unto you, He that heareth my word, and believeth on him that sent me, hath everlasting life, and shall not come into condemnation; but is passed from death unto life - John 5:24

The verities of Christianity are eternal in nature; salvation, justification, the seal of the Spirit, and all that God offers in Christ Jesus are eternal/forever. Hence, the believers' realities; his status and possession, in Christ are forever.

The writer of Hebrews often used the term forever, eternal, perfect to affirm the permanent nature of Christ's work and what God accomplished in Christ Jesus.

[10] For it became him, for whom are all things, and by whom are all things, in bringing many sons unto glory, to make the captain of their salvation ***perfect*** *through sufferings.* - Hebrews 2:10

[9] And being made ***perfect****, he became the author of* ***eternal*** *salvation unto all them that obey him;* - Hebrews 5:9

[14] How much more shall the blood of Christ, who through the ***eternal*** *Spirit offered himself without spot to God, purge your*

conscience from dead works to serve the living God?

[15] And for this cause he is the mediator of the new testament, that by means of death, for the redemption of the transgressions that were under the first testament, they which are called might receive the promise of ***eternal*** *inheritance.* - Hebrews 9:14-15

[12] But this man, after he had offered one sacrifice for sins ***for ever****, sat down on the right hand of God;*

[14] For by one offering he hath ***perfected for ever*** *them that are sanctified.* - Hebrews 10:12,14

All God has to offer in Christ are not for a while, they are everlasting. God's gift in Christ are for all time and eternity. The salvation God offers in Christ is forever, Jesus is the author of eternal salvation. He perfected, forever, them that are sanctified, hence, the believer has an eternal inheritance.

[22] By so much was Jesus made a surety of a better testament.

[23 And they truly were many priests, because they were not suffered to continue by reason of death:

[24 this man*, because he continueth ever, hath an unchangeable priesthood.*

[25] Wherefore he is able also to save them to the uttermost that come unto God by him, seeing he ever liveth to make intercession for them. - Hebrews 7:22-25

The writer of Hebrews, in context, made a contrast between the priesthood of the old covenant, the Levitical priesthood, and the new covenant, the Jesus priesthood. Recall we have earlier established that in the old covenant they had the high priest who offered animal sacrifice for the atonement of the sin of the children of Israel (Leviticus 16). However, in the new covenant, Jesus is both the sacrifice (offering) and the high priest (offeror).

[1] For every high priest taken from among men is ordained for

men in things pertaining to God, that he may offer both gifts and sacrifices for sins: - Hebrews 5:1

For every high priest is ordained to offer gifts and sacrifices: wherefore it is of necessity that this man have somewhat also to offer. - Hebrews 8:3

[20] Whither the forerunner is for us entered, even Jesus, made an high priest for ever after the order of Melchisedec. - Hebrews 6:20

The above texts explain the office of the priests, which is to offer sacrifices on behalf of others (sinners). Hence, Jesus in the offering of himself, therefore becomes our high priest in the new covenant. His priesthood is a post-resurrection reality. Recall we established in an earlier chapter that Jesus offered his life in heaven, so his high priesthood was when he went to heaven and offered himself.

[5] And he shall take of the congregation of the children of Israel two kids of the goats for a sin offering, and one ram for a burnt offering.

[6] And Aaron shall offer his bullock of the sin offering, which is for himself, and make an atonement for himself, and for his house.

[7] And he shall take the two goats, and present them before the LORD at the door of the tabernacle of the congregation.

[8] And Aaron shall cast lots upon the two goats; one lot for the LORD, and the other lot for the scapegoat. note

[9] And Aaron shall bring the goat upon which the LORD'S lot fell, and offer him for a sin offering

[10] But the goat, on which the lot fell to be the scapegoat, shall be presented alive before the LORD, to make an atonement with him, and to let him go for a scapegoat into the wilderness. - Leviticus 16:5-10

[22] Ye shall therefore keep all my statutes, and all my judgments, and do them: that the land, whither I bring you to dwell therein, spue you not out.

[24] But I have said unto you, Ye shall inherit their land, and I will give it unto you to possess it, a land that floweth with milk and honey: I am the LORD your God, which have separated you from other people. Leviticus 20: 22 , 24

In the old covenant, the high priest offers animal sacrifice yearly for the atonement of the sins of himself and the people. They make an offering of two goats. One goat was offered to make atonement for the sins of the children of Israel, while the second goat was to symbolize the removal of sin from the people. They foreshadow Jesus' death, burial, and resurrection. Notice, there is the goat sacrificed as a sin offering and there is the scapegoat presented alive. They both prefigure Jesus' offering. Jesus is the same who died as the "sin offering" and presented/offered himself alive in heaven for us. Jesus functioned as the priest and the offering, unlike in the old covenant. (Hebrews 9:14)

Also worthy of note is the yearly offering for sins in the old covenant, unlike Jesus' priesthood.

[1] For the law having a shadow of good things to come, and not the very image of the things, can never with those sacrifices which they offered year by year continually make the comers thereunto perfect.

[11] And every priest standeth daily ministering and offering oftentimes the same sacrifices, which can never take away sins: - Hebrew 10:1,11

[26] For such an high priest became us, who is holy, harmless, undefiled, separate from sinners, and made higher than the heavens;

[27] Who needeth not daily, as those high priests, to offer up sacrifice, first for his own sins, and then for the people's: for this he did once, when he offered up himself. Hebrews - 7:26-27

Clearly from the texts of scriptures above, Jesus' offering was done once because it was a perfect offering, the sacrifice of Jesus takes away sins forever. Hence, he sat at the right hand of the father as a result of his offering.

11] And every priest standeth daily ministering and offering oftentimes the same sacrifices, which can never take away sins:

[14] For by one offering he hath perfected for ever them that are sanctified - Hebrews 10:11-14

Under the law/the old covenant, the priests stand daily to offer sacrifices unlike Jesus. Also, the old covenant sacrifices could not take away sins because what they were doing was not perfect.

[11] *If therefore perfection were by the Levitical priesthood, (for under it the people received the law,) what further need was there that another priest should rise after the order of Melchisedec, and not be called after the order of Aaron?*

[19] For the law made nothing perfect, but the bringing in of a better hope did; by the which we draw nigh unto God - Hebrews 7:11,19

The high priests also was not perfect, so, they offered sacrifices for their own sins, and then for the people.

[1] For every high priest taken from among men is ordained for men in things pertaining to God, that he may offer both gifts and sacrifices for sins:

[2] Who can have compassion on the ignorant, and on them that are out of the way; for that he himself also is compassed with infirmity.

[3] And by reason hereof he ought, as for the people, so also for himself, to offer for sins. Hebrews 5:1-3

If the high priests of the Old Covenant had to offer animal sacrifices for themselves as well as the people, then it suffices to say that the office is imperfect and cannot save because the priests will also require a sacrifice for themselves. Hence, the sacrifice and the priesthood is imperfect, unlike Jesus' offering and priesthood.

While Jesus' offering was done once, and his priesthood work did not stop. After once and for all offering himself, Jesus sits alive forever to make intercession for the believer (Hebrews 8:1, Hebrews 7:25). Hence, the responsibility of salvation for the believer is that of the savior. In his letter, Paul spoke of Jesus' intercessory work.

[31] What shall we then say to these things? If God be for us, who can be against us?

[32] He that spared not his own Son, but delivered him up for us all, how shall he not with him also freely give us all things?

[33] Who shall lay any thing to the charge of God's elect? It is God that justifieth.

[34] Who is he that condemneth? It is Christ that died, yea rather, that is risen again, who is even at the right hand of God, who also maketh intercession for us.

[35] Who shall separate us from the love of Christ? shall tribulation, or distress, or persecution, or

famine, or nakedness, or peril, or sword?

[36] As it is written, For thy sake we are killed all the day long; we are accounted as sheep for the slaughter.

[37] Nay, in all these things we are more than conquerors through him that loved us.

[38] For I am persuaded, that neither death, nor life, nor angels, nor principalities, nor powers, nor things present, nor things to come,

[39] Nor height, nor depth, nor any other creature, shall be able to separate us from the love of God, which is in Christ Jesus our Lord.
Romans 8:31-39

Paul taught that Jesus' intercessory work is for God's elect, referring to those who have believed the gospel, and he said nothing can separate them from the love of God. Jesus continues his priestly ministry by sitting alive to make intercession for the believer.

The responsibility of saving and keeping a man saved is with Jesus. He keeps the believer from falling.

[24] Now unto him that is able to keep you from falling, and to present you faultless before the presence of his glory with exceeding joy, - Jude 24

[23] And the very God of peace sanctify you wholly; and I pray God your whole spirit and soul and body be preserved blameless unto the coming of our Lord Jesus Christ.

[24] Faithful is he that calleth you, who also will do it. - 1 Thessalonians 5:23-24,

[25] Husbands, love your wives, even as Christ also loved the church, and gave himself for it;

[26]That he might sanctify and cleanse it with the washing of water by the word,

[27] That he might present it to himself a glorious church, not having spot, or wrinkle, or any such thing; but that it should be holy and without blemish. - Ephesians 5:25-27

A believer cannot keep what he has not earned, so it is not in the believers' hands to keep his salvation but Christs.

Having said that, unlike salvation, spiritual growth is neither free nor is it God's responsibility. It is more of man's responsibility, and it requires effort from man. However, it is never an attempt to keep salvation.

Spiritual growth is the pursuit of development in other to enjoy the benefits embedded in salvation and walk in the light of the finished work of Christ.

Often times, believers have had themselves respond to alter calls to be saved time without number because they doubt their salvation and thus see themselves as "once saved" but now "unsaved" probably due to their unseemly conduct. This doublemindedness is usually a result of a lack of understanding between salvation and spiritual growth.

Salvation is God's work and Christ is the intercessor, guarantor, and saviour of the believer. Nothing can ever separate the believer from God's love for him in Christ. Even when we fall short, Jesus intercedes and guarantees our salvation.

Salvation is the state where a man is called righteous, forgiven, holy, and blameless because of what Jesus has done. It is not an automatic change of lifestyle or conduct. The process of change in a man's lifestyle or conduct reveals if he is growing spiritually or not.

Christian growth is measured by the degree to which the believer expresses the new life he has already received, not by an attempt to become more of what the believer is in Christ. It is about believers walking in the realities of their status and possession in Christ, which will only be possible when the believer feeds on those realities of their possession in Christ. As a believer gets his mind renewed, focusing on his realities, he will begin to experience transformation in his mind, which by extension will reflect in his conduct. Hence, spiritual growth is basically a growth in the mind.

Spiritual development is a function of knowledge, however, not just any knowledge, but the knowledge of Christ; what He has done for us and what He is doing in and through us.

And be not conformed to this world: but be ye transformed by the renewing of your mind, that ye may prove what is that good, and acceptable, and perfect, will of God. - Romans 12:2

But grow in grace, and in the knowledge of our Lord and Saviour Jesus Christ. To him be glory both now and for ever. Amen - 2 Peter 3:18

As Christ is being revealed, the believer gets to see himself in Christ because he is identified with Christ and, as a result, has the same identity as Christ.

Because the believer has been made to drink into one Spirit and thus engrafted into Christ's body, he sees himself in Christ as he beholds Christ, and the extent to which the believer appreciates in his mind the good things in him in Christ Jesus (his identity in Christ) is the extent to which he will experience active and effective Christian living.

[6] That the communication of thy faith may become effectual by the acknowledging of every good thing which is in you in Christ Jesus. - Philemon 1:6

This further reinforced that spiritual growth is primarily by knowledge. Hence, the prayers of the early Apostles focused on believers' understanding of who they are in Christ, what they can do in Christ, and what Christ can do through them *(Ephesians 1:18-21, 3:14-22, Philippians 1:9-11, Colossians 1:9-11, Philemon 1:6).*

While salvation is instant, Spiritual growth is not. Spiritual growth is progressive and rests on a continuous reception of the word. Since the understanding of the word does not happen instantaneously, like salvation, so also our spiritual growth. Spiritual maturity largely depends on our growth or understanding in the word. Hence, Apostle Paul's prayer focuses on insight into God's word.

Faith in the gospel makes a man a new creature. Instant changes occur and a new man emerges the moment a man believes in the gospel, however, his habits are being changed.

[17] Therefore if any man be in Christ, he is a new creature: old things are passed away; behold, all things are become new. - 2 Corinthians 5:17

The Christian lifestyle does not come automatically the day a man is saved. The lifestyle simply comes as growth in the word happens. Hence, it is first a change in the mind, then a change happens in his lifestyle.

While salvation costs a man nothing, Spiritual growth, on the other hand, will cost a man his time and consistent effort. Spiritual growth is never accidental; it cannot be effortless, and so it must have a consistent effort applied in the right direction.

Spiritual growth is deliberate, gradual, and measurable. Nobody just wakes up and discovers he has grown. There is an attitude that attracts it. However, spiritual growth is not a pursuit of justification or an attempt to earn the favor of God. All of these are the believer's possessions in Christ by faith in the gospel.

[1] Therefore being justified by faith, we have peace with God through our Lord Jesus Christ: - Romans 5:1

The believer is not to try to do what Christ has already done, an attempt to do such will be effort in the wrong direction. Spiritual growth will come when the believer is focused on his right and privileges in Christ, taking advantage of the same hence an effort in the right direction will be to consistently feed on Christ.

Spiritual growth comes from a Christ centered focus, and will produce a Christ centered life. No man can live the Christian life, the Christian life is received.

[12] Wherefore, my beloved, as ye have always obeyed, not as in my presence only, but now much more in my absence, work out your own salvation with fear and trembling.

[13] For it is God which worketh in you both to will and to do of his good pleasure. - Philippians 2:12-13

Observe from the text above, Apostle Paul never said "work for your salvation". No man can do that; any attempt to work for salvation is only a waste of time and effort, because only faith in Christ saves. Paul simply gives an instruction for believers to work out salvation, and it is important to note that his emphasis was on God working in us to do his will and pleasure. God working in the believer is Christ working in the believer, and Christ in the believer is by the Spirit of God in the believer.

[27] To whom God would make known what is the riches of the glory of this mystery among the Gentiles; which is Christ in you, the hope of glory: - Colossians 1:27

[8] So then they that are in the flesh cannot please God.

[9] But ye are not in the flesh, but in the Spirit, if so be that the Spirit of God dwell in you. Now if any man have not the Spirit of Christ, he is none of his.

[10] And if Christ be in you, the body is dead because of sin; but the Spirit is life because of righteousness. - Romans 8:8-10

The reason for Christian living is Christ in the believer. Christ lives through the believer, hence, the believer is to depend on the presence of Christ, within, to live the Christian life, and this he will do by focusing on the Word (his realities in Christ). Philippians 2:13

[6] As ye have therefore received Christ Jesus the Lord, so walk ye in him: - Colossians 2:6

No one should struggle to live the Christian life because coming with the new birth (Salvation) is the life of Christ which gives the ability to produce good works.

[10] For we are his workmanship, created in Christ Jesus unto good works, which God hath before ordained that we should walk in them - Ephesians 2:10

A consistent effort of feeding the mind with the word helps the believer to give expression to the life of Christ without struggle.

Spiritual growth is not a growth of the spirit, spirits do not grow. Spiritual growth is the development of the mind in the knowledge of Christ resulting in an outward transformation in our daily living.

God's Word is very fundamental to the Christian growth (2 Peter 3:18, 1 Peter 2:2, Acts 2:32). Desiring to be taught and fed with Christ is the first step to growing spiritually and this is what the local church is meant for. God has appointed elders in the local church to be responsible for feeding and overseeing the lifes of other believers.

[11] And he gave some, apostles; and some, prophets; and some, evangelists; and some, pastors and teachers;

[12] For the perfecting of the saints, for the work of the ministry, for the edifying of the body of Christ:

[13] Till we all come in the unity of the faith, and of the knowledge of

the Son of God, unto a perfect man, unto the measure of the stature of the fulness of Christ: note

[14] That we henceforth be no more children, tossed to and fro, and carried about with every wind of doctrine, by the sleight of men, and cunning craftiness, whereby they lie in wait to deceive; - Ephesians 4:11-14

[27] To whom God would make known what is the riches of the glory of this mystery among the Gentiles; which is Christ in you, the hope of glory - Colossians 1:27

The elders are to present every man perfect (mature) in Christ Jesus. Hence, recognition of the ministry gift and the local church is key to Christian growth. We have examined this in the previous chapter.

Spiritual growth is deliberate; it does not jump on a man, it is a choice. Spiritual growth requires a deliberate decision to want to submit oneself to the word. Spiritual growth will demand your time, zeal, and willingness. It will require a readjustment of priorities, a change of association, a change of local church in order to fellowship around people you want to be like. It will take time and effort to labor in the word and in prayer. Spiritual growth is not for comfort lovers; it demands intense devotion. A casual devotion will only produce a casual believer.

[11] Never be lacking in zeal, but keep your spiritual fervor, serving the Lord. - Romans 12:11 (NIV)

So Paul, here, instructs believers to keep the fire burning and not be lacking in zeal, but rather be diligent to maintain the glow and keep their spiritual fervor so they can keep serving the lord enthusiastically, as it is impossible to be active and alive spiritually and be apathetic in serving the lord. The cure for spiritual apathy is a consistent life of devotion to the study and the meditation of the word and prayer.

One of the proofs that a believer is growing is that he becomes effective in the sharing of his faith and he brings forth fruit. However, it is also possible to have believers whose sharing of their faith is inactive. Such believers are passive about their Christian life, yielding no fruit. (Philemon 1:4-6

Certain activities must be consistently and devotedly pursued by a believer if he is to continue growing and bearing fruit in his Christian walk.

A believer who desires to be effective must be found giving to these two necessary daily spiritual activities: study and meditation on God's word and prayer.

STUDYING AND MEDITATION OF THE WORD

As believers, we have instructions, from scriptures, to study and meditate on the word

[15] Study to shew thyself approved unto God, a workman that needeth not to be ashamed, rightly dividing the word of truth. - 2 Timothy 2:15

Study here implies diligence; it is to make an intense effort. Hence, Paul's instruction to Timothy (a disciple of Paul) clearly revealed that bible study requires diligence and carefulness so it can be presented to others with accuracy and void of errors, because if scriptures can be rightly divided (interpreted), then they can be wrongly interpreted also, so as Christ's disciples who have received Christ's ministry (2 Corinthians 5:17-19, Matthew 28:18-20). Paul's instruction is also applicable to you (all believers), so every believer must be diligent in their approach to the study of the word. Upon being taught in the local church, the believer must yet study and meditate upon that which he has been taught, further investigating thoroughly through scriptures. This further helps his understanding as well as deepens his convictions in the truth of God's word.

[10] And the brethren immediately sent away Paul and Silas by night unto Berea: who coming thither went into the synagogue of the Jews.

[11] These were more noble than those in Thessalonica, in that they received the word with all readiness of mind, and searched the scriptures daily, whether those things were so.

[12] Therefore many of them believed; also of honourable women which were Greeks, and of men, not a few. Acts 17:10-12

The folks who had the Apostles reach out to them in Berea were said to be noble in that, daily, they further investigated the scriptures for themselves after they were taught by the Apostles, and as a result, many of them were persuaded. A believer will not be persuasive about his faith if he has a poor study culture, and such believer can be a prey to false teachers.

[13] Till I come, give attendance to reading, to exhortation, to doctrine.

[14] Neglect not the gift that is in thee, which was given thee by prophecy, with the laying on of the hands of the presbytery.

[15] Meditate upon these things; give thyself wholly to them; that thy profiting may appear to all.

[16] Take heed unto thyself, and unto the doctrine; continue in them: for in doing this thou shalt both save thyself, and them that hear thee - 1 Timothy 4:13-16

Paul here gave Timothy an instruction to meditate on the word, and he revealed that profiting would then come afterwards. If meditation is profiting to Timothy, then it is to all believers, hence this instruction is applicable to every believer today. Take note that Timothy is to meditate on the doctrine and teaching that he has taught him; then his profiting would appear unto all. This again implies that there are boundaries to that which the believer should meditate upon. Believers are not to meditate on human opinions, ideas, or experiences to grow spiritually, but on the word, sound doctrine, and apostolic explanations. This is what brings about spiritual growth.

As a believer meditates on sound doctrine, he has his mind renewed and he experiences transformation in his earthly walk. Meditation is to ponder on something; it is the opposite of worry. When a man is worried, he begins to think, laboring in his mind. When it comes to meditation too, you apply your mind to it.

In meditation, we will have our thoughts and minds fixed on what is read and heard. It is through meditation that we receive understanding of the word we have received either by reading or hearing. It is not enough to read or hear the word. As important as it is to hear and read the word, it is also important to meditate on the word.

[8] This book of the law shall not depart out of thy mouth; but thou shalt ***meditate therein day and night****, that thou mayest observe to do according to all that is written therein: for then thou shalt make thy way prosperous, and then thou shalt have good success.* - Joshua 1:8

Meditation is the vehicle of understanding. Understanding comes via meditation.

[1] Blessed is the man that walketh not in the counsel of the ungodly, nor standeth in the way of sinners, nor sitteth in the seat of the

scornful.

[2] But his delight is in the law of the LORD; and in his law doth he ***meditate day and night.***

[3]And he shall be like a tree planted by the rivers of water, that bringeth forth his fruit in his season; his leaf also shall not wither; and whatsoever he doeth shall prosper. - Psalms 1:1-3

Notice the phrase 'day and night' from both texts. It implies: daily, regularly, consistently, hence, meditation should be what a believer deliberately attends to regularly.

Regular meditation on the word is a major way of keeping the mind, and guarding the heart from worldly influences and ideologies.

[23] Keep thy heart with all diligence; for out of it are the issues of life. - Proverbs 4:23

The mind is a very important part of a man, and it must be guarded with all diligence. The reason some people will suffer in hell is because of their minds.

[4] In whom the god of this world hath blinded the minds of them which believe not, lest the light of the glorious gospel of Christ, who is the image of God, should shine unto them. - 2 Corinthians 4:4

[17] This I say therefore, and testify in the Lord, that ye henceforth walk not as other Gentiles walk, in the vanity of their mind, - Ephesians 4:17

It is important and necessary that we learn to guard our reasoning because the mind is where spiritual growth takes place. The mind is where the believer walks in the spirit, and he walks in love; hence, the need to guard it by constantly feeding and meditating on the word. While the believer is not of this world, he however lives in this world and thus have "worldly" colleagues at work, school and as such he might have his mind exposed to corrupt influences from them, it could even be from the television and several other things, however, As a believer keeps his mind busy, by reflecting and thinking on the word regularly, he avoids having wrong information settle.

Feeding and meditating on the word is the way to have our thoughts remoulded, and aligned with God's word which consequently leads to transformation without.

[2] And be not conformed to this world: but be ye transformed by the renewing of your mind, that ye may prove what is that good, and acceptable, and perfect, will of God. - Romans 12:2

That transformation is the profiting that appears to all. This is what Paul calls a result of meditation on the things he taught; sound doctrine.

Notice, this 'profiting' appears to men, not God, hence the actions of the believers are necessarily not for God but for men. Man is already complete in Christ, there is nothing more that he is required to do in other to be complete. He is the workmanship of God in Christ.

[10] For we are his workmanship, created in Christ Jesus unto good works, which God hath before ordained that we should walk in them.- Ephesians 2:10

Transformation implies a change from within to the outside. It is a developmental stage of growth that happens as believers have their minds renewed with the word. However, this transformation is not changing to become anything more than what the believer already is. Upon salvation, the believer already experienced transformation, and he is perfect in Christ; he is already everything he will ever be, so the transformation Paul meant is the believer giving expression to his nature, that is, the believer simply living out who he already is, reflecting his changed nature in his conduct.

The man in Christ is born of the spirit of God and thus alive in the spirit, he is in the spirit and the spirit is in him.

[9] But ye are not in the flesh, but in the Spirit, if so be that the Spirit of God dwell in you. Now if any man have not the Spirit of Christ, he is none of his.

[10] And if Christ be in you, the body is dead because of sin; but the Spirit is life because of righteousness.

[11] But if the Spirit of him that raised up Jesus from the dead dwell in you, he that raised up Christ from the dead shall also quicken your mortal bodies by his Spirit that dwelleth in you.

[12] Therefore, brethren, we are debtors, not to the flesh, to live after the flesh.

[13] For if ye live after the flesh, ye shall die: but if ye through the Spirit do mortify the deeds of the body, ye shall live.

[14] For as many as are led by the Spirit of God, they are the sons of God.

[15] For ye have not received the spirit of bondage again to fear; but ye have received the Spirit of adoption, whereby we cry, Abba, Father.

[16] The Spirit itself beareth witness with our spirit, that we are the children of God: - Romans 8:9-16

The Spirit resident in the believer is reason he can now call God his father. It is how he is engrafted into the family of God, hence, he is in union with the Father in Christ by the spirit indwelling him.

[13] For by one Spirit are we all baptized into one body, whether we be Jews or Gentiles, whether we be bond or free; and have been all

made to drink into one Spirit. - 1 Corinthians 12:13

The believer has been made to drink into one Spirit. The believer is in the Spirit and he is to walk in the Spirit.

[22] But the fruit of the Spirit is love, joy, peace, longsuffering, gentleness, goodness, faith,

[25] If we live in the Spirit, let us also walk in the Spirit. - Galatians 5:22,25

To walk in the spirit simply means to conduct or regulate oneself, ways, thoughts, and life patterns from his Spirit. This is so because he is alive in the Spirit, and so he is instructed to continue in the Spirit. That is the way he got saved and he is to keep living the same way. Since he has experienced transformation, has been made holy, and righteous, then he is to continue living out that transformed, sanctified, and righteous life. Spiritual growth will now be seen primarily through his thoughts and consequently action.

A believer living by the influence of the word (the Spirit) is one who is growing spiritually, hence, the growth of a believer depends on his attendance to the study and meditation of the word.

[22] But be ye doers of the word, and not hearers only, deceiving your own selves.

[23] For if any be a hearer of the word, and not a doer, he is like unto a man beholding his natural face in a glass:

[24] For he beholdeth himself, and goeth his way, and straightway forgetteth what manner of man he was.

[25] But whoso looketh into the perfect law of liberty, and continueth therein, he being not a forgetful hearer, but a doer of the work, this man shall be blessed in his deed. - James 1:22-25

James, in this text, is instructing believers to do the word. However, he is showing us that hearing the word precedes doing the word. James used "natural face" to refer to the way the believer is born, that is, the face of his birth. The word glass implies a mirror which explains the word reflecting who the believer is to him. So James, in verse 22, reveals that a man who hears the word without doing the same is deceiving himself. To decieve here implies to live a lie; to live in deception, delusion, hence, James is explaining that a believer who does not do the word is acting besides himself, such believer is living a lie; presenting another image about himself. This is so because James had earlier explained that the believer is begotten of God by the word.

[18] Of his own will begat he us with the word of truth, that we should be a kind of firstfruits of his creatures.

[22] But be ye doers of the word, and not hearers only, deceiving your own selves.

[23] For if any be a hearer of the word, and not a doer, he is like unto a man beholding his natural face in a glass:

[24] For he beholdeth himself, and goeth his way, and straightway forgetteth what manner of man he was.

[25] But whoso looketh into the perfect law of liberty, and continueth therein, he being not a forgetful hearer, but a doer of the work, this man shall be blessed in his deed. - James 1:18,22-25

This implies that believers will find their identity in the word only. To live not according to the word (the reality of who he is in the word) is to live a lie.

Hence the epistles' prayer focus for believers is concerning the knowledge of the word.

(Eph 1:17-21, Eph 3:16-19, Phil 1:9-11, Col 1:9-11, Phil 1:6)

Noteworthy is James' emphasis on being a hearer of the word. James in v24-25 further revealed that the reason a man will hear the word and not do the word is because he forgets the manner of man he was. He forgot about the man he saw in the mirror of the word. While the one who hears and does the word is because he continued to look into the mirror of the word. So the believer will not struggle to do the word when he focuses his attention on the word (his realities in Christ).

This is the same thing Paul explained in Gal 5:22, 25 as walking in the spirit. The difference between the doer and the hearer only is that the hearer only who is not doing the word stops looking. Notice that the one who does the word did nothing extra; he simply kept looking, so being a forgetful hearer is not necessarily that you forget the Scriptures but that you stopped looking, you stopped being conscious of your realities in Christ, while the man who looks intently and continues, the same is blessed in his deeds (actions).

[3] For this is the love of God, that we keep his commandments: and his commandments are not grievous. 1 John 5:3

Grevious here would mean an addition, something that is weighty, heavy or burdensome. John revealed that God's commands are not burdensome to the believer; they are not weighty to the believer. The instructons in the word are natural to the believer. God has not instructed the believer to do what he has not given the ability to do. Hence the word to the believer is first a revelation before it becomes an instruction. That is why Paul's prayer was for revelation. It is so we will see and know. So, when the word is read, the believer must begin to see himself.

The believer is not studying to become, but rather studying the word in order for his reality to be expressed through him. As the believer devotes himself to meditating on the reality of who he is in Christ, unconsciously, that reality becomes his reality.

As E.W Kenyon of blessed memory says, "When we get to know who we are in Christ, as believers, we unconsciously practice it."

The approach of the epistles to spiritual growth in the understanding and consciousness of who the believer is in Christ and the consequent influence on his actions and conduct is therefore important to Christian growth.

PRAYER

Prayer is an act of making known our request to God. It is to express our desires to God via words. Hence, it cannot be done by thinking. Words have to be spoken.

[24] Therefore I say unto you, What things soever ye desire, when ye pray, believe that ye receive them, and ye shall have them. - Mark 11:24,

[6] Be careful for nothing; but in every thing by prayer and supplication with thanksgiving let your requests be made known unto God. - Philippians 4:6

Brethren, my heart's ***desire and prayer*** *to God for Israel is, that they might be saved.* - Romans 10:1

However, beyond making requests or expressing our desires to God, prayer for the believer is much more of a fellowship with his father. It is a discussion based on relationship; it is a way the believer communes with their father. Hence, prayer should not be reactionary; that is, when there is a desire or need, then I go to pray; or when there is a problem, a challenge, then I go to pray. Prayer for the believer should be a lifestyle. The believer must be found praying regularly and effectively, hence the instruction for the believer to pray ceaselessly all through the epistles.

[12] Rejoicing in hope; patient in tribulation; ***continuing instant in prayer****;* - Romans 12:12

Prayer is to be done continuously which implies there will never be a time prayer will be unnecessary.

[18] Praying always *with all prayer and supplication in the Spirit, and watching thereunto with all perseverance and supplication for all saints;* - Ephesians 6:18

[2] Continue in prayer*, and watch in the same with thanksgiving;* - Colossians 4:2

[17] Pray without ceasing. - 1Thessalonians 5:17

Noteworthy are the terms Paul used for prayers: 'praying always", "continue in prayer", "pray without ceasing". All of these suggest that prayer ought to be a regular feature in a Christian lifestyle. It is a constant and it has no season. Its season is always. A believer who is not given to regular prayer is one living in disobedience because consistency in prayer is an Apostolic instruction, not a suggestion to the believer.

Jesus remains the ultimate discipler of all believers and every believer ought to be a follower of Christ. Hence, His conduct and His lifestyle while on earth are examples for believers to follow today.

[6] He that saith he abideth in him ought himself also so to walk, even as he walked. - 1 John 2:6

[1] Be ye therefore followers of God, as dear children;

[2] And walk in love, as Christ also hath loved us, and hath given

himself for us an offering and a sacrifice to God for a sweetsmelling savour. - Ephesians 5:1-2

As God's children, we are to be His imitators, and the way we understand God is through Christ. Christ is God's explanation to the believer.

[18] No man hath seen God at any time; the only begotten Son, which is in the bosom of the Father, he hath declared him. - John 1:18.

We imitate God by imitating Christ, **hence we will examine Jesus prayer life while he was on the earth,**

[35] And in the morning, rising up a great while before day, he went out, and departed into a solitary place, and there prayed. Mark 1:35,

Jesus rose early in the morning to pray. It is what a man values the most that he first attends to in the day. Jesus will often rise to pray before he starts his day. That is an example for believers to follow today.

[23] And when he had sent the multitudes away, he went up into a mountain apart to pray: and when the evening was come, he was there alone. Matt. 14:23

Notice that Jesus in the evening again separates himself to pray. So Jesus will start his day with prayer and finish it with the same.

[12] And it came to pass in those days, that he went out into a mountain to pray, and continued all night in prayer to God. Luke 6:12

Again, Jesus was said to have separated himself to pray all night.

Jesus had all night prayers. In the Jewish culture, night begins by 6pm and day breaks by 6am, hence Jesus praying all night would mean he prayed for 12 hours, spending all the night praying. This is the pattern of Chrisian living Jesus left for the believers today

[2] And when he had fasted forty days and forty nights, he was afterward an hungred. Matt. 4:2,

Jesus, before he began his ministry, went to the wilderness and fasted for forty days and nights. He must have spent quality time praying also, as his custom was.

[38] For this is my blood of the new testament, which is shed for many for the remission of sins.

[42] He went away again the second time, and prayed, saying, O my Father, if this cup may not pass away from me, except I drink it, thy will be done. Matt 26:38, 42,

On the night before his crucifixion, Jesus was again found praying, so just as he started His ministry with prayers, Jesus ended it with prayers also.

[28] And it came to pass about an eight days after these sayings, he took Peter and John and James, and went up into a mountain to pray.

[29] And as he prayed, the fashion of his countenance was altered, and his raiment was white and glistering.

[30] And, behold, there talked with him two men, which were Moses and Elias:

[31] Who appeared in glory, and spake of his decease which he should accomplish at Jerusalem.

[32] But Peter and they that were with him were heavy with sleep: and when they were awake, they saw his glory, and the two men that stood with him.

[33] And it came to pass, as they departed from him, Peter said unto Jesus, Master, it is good for us to be here: and let us make three tabernacles; one for thee, and one for Moses, and one for Elias: not knowing what he said.

[34] While he thus spake, there came a cloud, and overshadowed them: and they feared as they entered into the cloud.

[35] And there came a voice out of the cloud, saying, This is my beloved Son: hear him.

[36] And when the voice was past, Jesus was found alone. And they kept it close, and told no man in those days any of those things which they had seen.

[37] And it came to pass, that on the next day, when they were come down from the hill, much people met him.

[38] And, behold, a man of the company cried out, saying, Master, I beseech thee, look upon my son: for he is mine only child.

[42] And as he was yet a coming, the devil threw him down, and tare him. And Jesus rebuked the unclean spirit, and healed the child, and delivered him again to his father. Luke 9:28–38,42.

Before Jesus worked miracles, He prayed.

[12] And it came to pass, when he was in a certain city, behold a man full of leprosy: who seeing Jesus fell on his face, and besought him, saying, Lord, if thou wilt, thou canst make me clean.

[13] And he put forth his hand, and touched him, saying, I will: be thou clean. And immediately the leprosy departed from him.

[14] And he charged him to tell no man: but go, and shew thyself to the priest, and offer for thy cleansing, according as Moses commanded, for a testimony unto them.

[15] But so much the more went there a fame abroad of him: and great multitudes came together to hear, and to be healed by him of their infirmities.

[16] And he withdrew himself into the wilderness, and prayed. Luke

5:12-16.

After Jesus had worked miracles, He literally just finished a "major miracle crusade" where He had a great multitude in attendance healed supernaturally. Afterwards, Jesus withdrew himself, not to go rest first, but to pray.

[34] And Jesus, when he came out, saw much people, and was moved with compassion toward them, because they were as sheep not having a shepherd: and he began to teach them many things.

[35] And when the day was now far spent, his disciples came unto him, and said, This is a desert place, and now the time is far passed:

[41] And when he had taken the five loaves and the two fishes, he looked up to heaven, and blessed, and brake the loaves, and gave them to his disciples to set before them; and the two fishes divided he among them all.

[42] And they did all eat, and were filled.

[43] And they took up twelve baskets full of the fragments, and of the fishes.

[44] And they that did eat of the loaves were about five thousand men.

[45] And straightway he constrained his disciples to get into the ship, and to go to the other side before unto Bethsaida, while he sent away the people.

[46] And when he had sent them away, he departed into a mountain to pray. Mark 6:34–35, 41–46.

Here again, Jesus had just finished a "major teaching meeting" with several thousand mighty miracles wrought. He supernaturally made food available for about five thousand men. However, a notable fact about this event was that Jesus, after teaching all day, withdrew himself to go pray. He will always seize every available time for praying. If he is not ministering; preaching or teaching, then He will be praying. Jesus practiced a ceaseless prayer lifestyle. Little wonder the Apostles in their epistles instructed that believers also pray without ceasing. It is the culture Jesus passed across to them.

Jesus lived a consistent life of prayer. He was never too busy with preaching and teaching that he could not pray. Prayer was an important part of his life, so no one can claim to be a follower of Jesus and not value a regular praying culture. Obviously, Jesus' prayer life was the bedrock of His success in ministry.

Thus far, we have seen Jesus' devotion to prayer. He had a lifestyle and culture of prayer. Apparently, Jesus never made prayer a reaction, but rather a way of life. Jesus did not pray so he could do miracles. If that was the reason he prayed then, He needed not to withdraw Himself to pray again after doing miracles.

What could Jesus (being in flesh) be asking for that causes Him to be so ceaselessly devoted to prayer—obviously beyond expressing His desire to commune with the Father as a sign of devotion. Jesus is the perfect example for believers; he not only taught but also practiced prayer (Luke 11:1).

Jesus Himself taught His disciples how to pray based on the fact that He Himself was given to prayer, so He taught prayer by percept and by example. By precept is to teach the art of prayer: what it is, what it entails, while example refers to the very act of prayer, that is, to show by action.

Hence, Jesus did not just teach his disciples by precept; he took them to pray (Matt 26:36–38). It is not enough to know how to pray or understand perfectly the doctrine of prayer; it is more important to pray. If a man has not prayed, he has not prayed. Learning how to pray must never replace the act of praying itself.

Upon Jesus' resurrection, and ascension, His disciples/church were also given to prayer having learnt the art, and act from Him.

Then returned they unto Jerusalem from the mount called Olivet, which is from Jerusalem a sabbath day's journey.

[13] And when they were come in, they went up into an upper room, where abode both Peter, and James, and John, and Andrew, Philip, and Thomas, Bartholomew, and Matthew, James the son of Alphaeus, and Simon Zelotes, and Judas the brother of James.

*[14] These all **continued** with one accord in prayer and supplication, with the women, and Mary the mother of Jesus, and with his brethren.* - Acts 1:13-14

'Continued' here describes an attitude of consistency and perseverance.

[1] Now Peter and John went up together into the temple at the hour of prayer, being the ninth hour. - Acts3:1

Peter and John also separated themselves to pray.

[4] But we will give ourselves continually to prayer, and to the ministry of the word. - Acts 6:4

The apostles delegated natural responsibility so they can attend to prayer, they passed the same culture to their converts.

[5] Peter therefore was kept in prison: but prayer was made without ceasing of the church unto God for him. - Acts 12:5

The church, although persecuted, also prayed ceaselessly for Peter's deliverance.

[6] Whom they set before the apostles: and when they had prayed,

they laid their hands on them. - Acts 6:6

In appointing deacons, the apostles prayed.

The early church was also given to prayer, it was a necessary, and vital part of their activities. They practiced prayer individually, and collectively as a church.

Paul and Silas prayed when they were imprisoned.

[25] And at midnight Paul and Silas prayed, and sang praises unto God: and the prisoners heard them. – Acts 16:25

Paul prayed privately upon his conversion.

[11] And the Lord said unto him, Arise, and go into the street which is called Straight, and enquire in the house of Judas for one called Saul, of Tarsus: for, behold, he prayeth, - Acts 9:11

We will see Paul's devotion to prayer, as an individual, in his epistles.

[19] Because that which may be known of God is manifest in them; for God hath shewed it unto them. - Romans 1:19

[16] Cease not to give thanks for you, making mention of you in my prayers; - Ephesians 1:16

[8] For God is my record, how greatly I long after you all in the bowels of Jesus Christ. – Philippians 1:8

[9] For this cause we also, since the day we heard it, do not cease to pray for you, and to desire that ye might be filled with the knowledge of his will in all wisdom and spiritual understanding; - Colossians 1:9

[3] I thank God, whom I serve from my forefathers with pure conscience, that without ceasing I have remembrance of thee in my prayers night and day; - 2 Timothy 1:3

[13] For this cause also thank we God without ceasing, because, when ye received the word of God which ye heard of us, ye received it not as the word of men, but as it is in truth, the word of God, which

effectually worketh also in you that believe. - 1 Thessalonians 2:13

Peter also was given to prayer as an individual, He also had private moment of prayer.

[9] On the morrow, as they went on their journey, and drew nigh unto the city, Peter went up upon the housetop to pray about the sixth hour: - Acts 10:9

Evidently, Jesus, the apostles, and the early church were given to consistent prayer collectively, and privately, and there are plethora instructions left for the believers to pray in their epistles.

Prayer therefore is a necessity for every believer in Christ. The believer must be given to prayer meetings or prayer sessions in the local church and as we have established in earlier chapters, prayer is a core activity of the local church.

A believer should not be lackadaisical about his prayer life, he must have a personal prayer life because a regular praying culture is very important to the Christian growth.

Prayer, itself, is more important than the things we get from it. While it is a known fact that prayer changes things, situations, circumstances, and much more; there is absolutely nothing prayer cannot do and the believer who is given to prayer is one who is taking advantage of his authority, his rights and privileges in Christ. However, the most important thing that prayer changes is the believer himself. In prayer, believers fellowship around God's will, it is a place where the believers' thoughts, will, and desires are exchanged for God's thought and desires.

When the believer is given to prayer, he will begin to see with the eyes of God, God's plan and purpose will be laid bare before him. It is in prayers we are strenghtened to follow God's plan no matter how grievous it may look. Prayer makes Jesus giving up himself to die possible, If Jesus had not prayed his strength could have failed him.

[31] And the Lord said, Simon, Simon, behold, Satan hath desired to have you, that he may sift you as wheat:

[32] But I have prayed for thee, that thy faith fail not: and when thou art converted, strengthen thy brethren.

[33] And he said unto him, Lord, I am ready to go with thee, both into prison, and to death.

[34] And he said, I tell thee, Peter, the cock shall not crow this day, before that thou shalt thrice deny that thou knowest me. luke 22:31-34,

[34] Jesus said unto him, Verily I say unto thee, That this night, before the cock crow, thou shalt deny me thrice.

[35] Peter said unto him, Though I should die with thee, yet will I not deny thee. Likewise also said all the disciples.

[36] Then cometh Jesus with them unto a place called Gethsemane, and saith unto the disciples, Sit ye here, while I go and pray yonder.

[37] And he took with him Peter and the two sons of Zebedee, and began to be sorrowful and very heavy.

[38] Then saith he unto them, My soul is exceeding sorrowful, even unto death: tarry ye here, and watch with me.

[39] And he went a little farther, and fell on his face, and prayed, saying, O my Father, if it be possible, let this cup pass from me: nevertheless not as I will, but as thou wilt.

[40] And he cometh unto the disciples, and findeth them asleep, and saith unto Peter, What, could ye not watch with me one hour?

[41] Watch and pray, that ye enter not into temptation: the spirit indeed is willing, but the flesh is weak.

[42] He went away again the second time, and prayed, saying, O my Father, if this cup may not pass away from me, except I drink it, thy will be done.

[43] And he came and found them asleep again: for their eyes were heavy.

[44] And he left them, and went away again, and prayed the third time, saying the same words.

[45] Then cometh he to his disciples, and saith unto them, Sleep on now, and take your rest: behold, the hour is at hand, and the Son of man is betrayed into the hands of sinners. Matthew 26: 34-45

Prayer resets our priorities. Prayer changes our desires and places us on a pedestal of zeal. Prayer makes following God's plan easy, it makes the believer active, and it builds his capacity for effectiveness. Prayer makes the believer bold even in the face of persecution.

[17] And he taught, saying unto them, Is it not written, My house shall be called of all nations the house of prayer? but ye have made it a den of thieves. Mark 11:17

Jesus quoted Jeremiah's prophecy

[11] Is this house, which is called by my name, become a den of robbers in your eyes? Behold, even I have seen it, saith the Lord. Jeremiah 7:11

Isaiah also prophesied about this

[7]Before she travailed, she brought forth; before her pain came, she was delivered of a man child Isaiah 66:7

This prophecy was concerning the believer, the believer in Christ has become that house.

[5] Ye also, as lively stones, are built up a spiritual house, an holy priesthood, to offer up spiritual sacrifices, acceptable to God by Jesus

Christ.

[6] Wherefore also it is contained in the scripture, Behold, I lay in Sion a chief corner stone, elect, precious: and he that believeth on him shall not be confounded.

[7] Unto you therefore which believe he is precious: but unto them which be disobedient, the stone which the builders disallowed, the same is made the head of the corner,

[8] And a stone of stumbling, and a rock of offence, even to them which stumble at the word, being disobedient: whereunto also they were appointed.

[9] But ye are a chosen generation, a royal priesthood, an holy nation, a peculiar people; that ye should shew forth the praises of him who hath called you out of darkness into his marvellous light; 1 peter 2:5-9,

[21] In whom all the building fitly framed together groweth unto an holy temple in the Lord:

[22] In whom ye also are builded together for an habitation of God through the Spirit. Ephesians 2:21-22

So, when Jesus says my house shall be called the house of prayer, he is saying the believers (those he will indwell) shall be characterized and known for prayer. So the believer is the house of prayer today, and he is to be known for it.

"House of prayer", relatively used for the believer, is to indicate his character. Believers are to function as a house of prayer. It also implies that unlike the old testament, the believer need not go to the Temple to pray, he is not limited to any place of prayer as practiced under the old convenant. He can now pray at anytime and in any place. This will lead us into praying in the Spirit.

PRAYING IN THE SPIRIT

[18] Pray at all times (on every occasion, in every season) in the Spirit, with all [manner of] prayer and entreaty. To that end keep alert and watch with strong purpose and perseverance, interceding in behalf of all the saints (God's consecrated people). Ephesians 6:18 (amp)

The pattern for new testament prayer is to pray in the Spirit, Paul says all manner of request can be done in the spirit.

[14] For if I pray in an unknown tongue, my spirit prayeth, but my understanding is unfruitful.

[15] What is it then? I will pray with the spirit, and I will pray with the understanding also: I will sing with the spirit, and I will sing with the understanding also. - 1 Corinthians 14:14-15

In the text above Paul revealed that praying in the Spirit is praying in tongues, so the New testament pattern of prayer is to pray in the Spirit.

Tongues is the praying language of every believer and we must all speak with tongues because we have the ability. Tongues is part of the signs Jesus said will follow the believing ones(those who have believed the gospel).

[17] And these signs shall follow them that believe; In my name shall they cast out devils; they shall speak with new tongues; - Mark 16:17

Tongues is peculiar to the tribe of the forgiven, it is part of the inheritance of those who have believed the gospel.

Paul in his letter acknowledges he speaks with tongues more than the Corinthian church. Paul was a man given to praying in tongues

[18] I thank my God, I speak with tongues more than ye all: - 1

Corinthians 14:18

Speaking with tongues is the way believers commune the father.

[2] For he that speaketh in an unknown tongue speaketh not unto men, but unto God: for no man understandeth him; howbeit in the spirit he speaketh mysteries. - 1 Corinthians 14:2

Observe text above; tongues is not addressed to men, it is addressed to the father. Tongues serve a dual purpose; as believers communicate their desires to God via praying in tongues, they are, at the same time, building up or edifying himself

[2] For he that speaketh in an unknown tongue speaketh not unto men, but unto God: for no man understandeth him; howbeit in the spirit he speaketh mysteries.

[4] He that speaketh in an unknown tongue edifieth himself; but he that prophesieth edifieth the church.

[18] I thank my God, I speak with tongues more than ye all: - 1 Corinthians 14:2,4,18

[20] But ye, beloved, building up yourselves on your most holy faith, praying in the Holy Ghost, - Jude 1:20

The way to pray in the New testament is to pray in the Spirit because at the New birth, the Believer receives the Spirit indwelling and thus has the ability to pray at anytime and in any place. This is the advantage of praying in tongues.

GOD'S CHARACTER IN PRAYER

A salient issue that must be settled in our heart, if we must pray effectively, is God's character in prayer.

Apostle James gave a very detailed description of God's character in his letter.

[5] If any of you lack wisdom, let him ask of God, that giveth to all men liberally, and upbraideth not; and it shall be given him.

[6] But let him ask in faith, nothing wavering. For he that wavereth is like a wave of the sea driven with the wind and tossed.

[7] For let not that man think that he shall receive any thing of the Lord.

[8] A double minded man is unstable in all his ways. - James 1:5-8

Observe the words "liberally" and "upbraideth not" used for God's giving. Liberally implies singlemindedness or generosity, while "upbraideth not" implies not finding fault. James is explaining that God is singleminded when it comes to his giving in prayer. God gives generously without finding fault.

However, James in verse 8 explains that when a man is double-minded in his knowledge of God's character where giving in prayer is concerned, then such a man will not be effective in receiving in prayer. However, God's character remains the same. God gives all the time without finding fault.

WHAT TO PRAY FOR

It is not enough as a believer to obey the apostolic/scriptural instructions to pray regularly; it is equally important that we know and obey the Apostolic instructions on what our focus should be in prayer. Many a time, this aspect is disregarded because of the general assumption that everyone should know what to pray for; many assume that as long as there is a need, then I take it to God in prayer. Unbelievers, and several other religions, pray too; when there is a need or challenge, they pray; hence, their needs inform what they pray about. However, is this so with the way believers pray? The Scriptures remain the basis for our evidence and conviction on any subject matter, so we shall further examine this from the scriptures.

Believers are ultimately disciples of Christ, a believer is to follow his Pastor to the extent that he follows Christ

[1]Be ye followers of me, even as I also am of Christ. - 1 Corinthians 11:1

Christ remains the hallmark, the perfect model or example to follow.

Jesus was given to prayer in his earthly walk as we have earlier seen, we have several records of how he prayed, however only twice was his request in prayer recorded.

[39] And he went a little further, and fell on his face, and prayed, saying, O my Father, if it be possible, let this cup pass from me: nevertheless not as I will, but as thou wilt.

[40] And he cometh unto the disciples, and findeth them asleep, and saith unto Peter, What, could ye not watch with me one hour?

[41] Watch and pray, that ye enter not into temptation: the spirit indeed is willing, but the flesh is weak.

[42] He went away again the second time, and prayed, saying, O my Father, if this cup may not pass away from me, except I drink it, thy will be done.

[43] And he came and found them asleep again: for their eyes were heavy.

[44] And he left them, and went away again, and prayed the third time, saying the same words. - Matthew 26:39-44

This was just shortly before his crucifixion. His prayer was for God's will to be done, and in this context he was referring to his obedience to the point of death, his sacrifice for sins. It suffices to say Jesus' prayer focus was on matters that surround the prevalence of the gospel on the earth and the salvation of men.

John also captured Jesus' prayer request/focus in his letter

[9] I pray for them: I pray not for the world, but for them which thou hast given me; for they are thine.

[10] And all mine are thine, and thine are mine; and I am glorified in them.

[11] And now I am no more in the world, but these are in the world, and I come to thee. Holy Father, keep through thine own name those whom thou hast given me, that they may be one, as we are.

[12] While I was with them in the world, I kept them in thy name: those that thou gavest me I have kept, and none of them is lost, but the son of perdition; that the scripture might be fulfilled.

[13] And now come I to thee; and these things I speak in the world, that they might have my joy fulfilled in themselves.

[14] I have given them thy word; and the world hath hated them, because they are not of the world, even as I am not of the world.

[15] I pray not that thou shouldest take them out of the world, but that thou shouldest keep them from the evil.

[16] They are not of the world, even as I am not of the world.

[17] Sanctify them through thy truth: thy word is truth.

[18] As thou hast sent me into the world, even so have I also sent them into the world.

[19] And for their sakes I sanctify myself, that they also might be sanctified through the truth.

[20] Neither pray I for these alone, but for them also which shall believe on me through their word;

[21] That they all may be one; as thou, Father, art in me, and I in thee, that they also may be one in us: that the world may believe that thou hast sent me.

[22] And the glory which thou gavest me I have given them; that they may be one, even as we are one:

[23] I in them, and thou in me, that they may be made perfect in one; and that the world may know that thou hast sent me, and hast loved them, as thou hast loved me.

[24] Father, I will that they also, whom thou hast given me, be with me where I am; that they may behold my glory, which thou hast given me: for thou lovedst me before the foundation of the world.

[25] O righteous Father, the world hath not known thee: but I have known thee, and these have known that thou hast sent me.

[26] And I have declared unto them thy name, and will declare it: that the love wherewith thou hast loved me may be in them, and I in them. - John 17:9-26

Jesus' prayer here was for his disciples and those who would believe in him. His prayer focus here also was on ministry, woven around salvation and spiritual growth.

Apart from the fact that Jesus' desire to commune with the Father in prayer, his focus in prayer at every other time must have been on situations that surround the Gospel and its prevalence. Jesus could not have been about praying for his material needs. There is no record of such in the Scriptures. After all, he never owned a ride or house or "family" to himself while he walked the earth, yet he was devoted to prayer. This presupposes that prayer is beyond receiving things. Prayer on its own is a ministry. It is a ministry as long as it is for others.

Since prayer involves verbalizing our desires to God, Christ's desires can not be any different from God's ultimate desire.

[3]For this is good and acceptable in the sight of God our Saviour;

[4]Who will have all men to be saved, and to come unto the knowledge of the truth. - 1 Timothy 2:3-4

So it suffices to say Jesus focus in prayer must have been on situations that surrounds the Gospel.

Taking a lead from Jesus prayer ministry, we shall further consider the focus of the prayers of the Apostles in their Epistles

[1]Brethren, my heart's desire and prayer to God for Israel is, that they might be saved. - Romans 10:1

Paul prayed for the salvation of the nation of Israel

[16]Cease not to give thanks for you, making mention of you in my prayers;

[17]That the God of our Lord Jesus Christ, the Father of glory, may give unto you the spirit of wisdom and revelation in the knowledge of him:

[18]The eyes of your understanding being enlightened; that ye may know what is the hope of his calling, and what the riches of the glory of his inheritance in the saints,

[19]And what is the exceeding greatness of his power to us-ward who believe, according to the working of his mighty power,

[20]Which he wrought in Christ, when he raised him from the dead, and set him at his own right hand in the heavenly places, - Ephesians 1:16-20

Paul prayed for insight into God's word, and power for other believers. Again the prayer focus in the epistles was for spiritual growth of other believers. Other instances with similar request

[14]For this cause I bow my knees unto the Father of our Lord Jesus Christ,

[15]Of whom the whole family in heaven and earth is named,

[16]That he would grant you, according to the riches of his glory, to

be strengthened with might by his Spirit in the inner man;

[17]That Christ may dwell in your hearts by faith; that ye, being rooted and grounded in love,

[18]May be able to comprehend with all saints what is the breadth, and length, and depth, and height;

[19]And to know the love of Christ, which passeth knowledge, that ye might be filled with all the fulness of God. - Ephesians 3:14-19

[9]And this I pray, that your love may abound yet more and more in knowledge and in all judgment;

[10]That ye may approve things that are excellent; that ye may be sincere and without offence till the day of Christ;

[11]Being filled with the fruits of righteousness, which are by Jesus Christ, unto the glory and praise of God.

- Philippians 1:9-11

[6]That the communication of thy faith may become effectual by the acknowledging of every good thing which is in you in Christ Jesus. - Philemon 1:6

Paul also related Epaphras' commitment to praying for the believers in colosse for growth in the knowledge of Christ.

[12]Epaphras, who is one of you, a servant of Christ, saluteth you, always labouring fervently for you in prayers, that ye may stand perfect and complete in all the will of God. - Colossians 4:12

Paul also requested that the church pray for him as a Minister of the Gospel.

[18]Praying always with all prayer and supplication in the Spirit, and watching thereunto with all perseverance and supplication for all saints;

[19]And for me, that utterance may be given unto me, that I may open my mouth boldly, to make known the mystery of the gospel - Ephesians 6:18-19

Paul requested that the church pray for him to be bold to preach the gospel as he ought. This is similar to his request from the church in colosse too.

[2]Continue in prayer, and watch in the same with thanksgiving;

[3]Withal praying also for us, that God would open unto us a door of utterance, to speak the mystery of Christ, for which I am also in bonds: - Colossians 4:2-3

[30]Now I beseech you, brethren, for the Lord Jesus Christ's sake, and for the love of the Spirit, that ye strive together with me in your prayers to God for me;

[31]That I may be delivered from them that do not believe in Judaea; and that my service which I have for Jerusalem may be accepted of the saints; - Romans 15:30-31

We see Paul, again, requesting that the church pray for his deliverance and preservation in the course of preaching the gospel. Other similar instances where Paul made such request is:

[1]Finally, brethren, pray for us, that the word of the Lord may have free course, and be glorified, even as it is with you:

[2]And that we may be delivered from unreasonable and wicked men: for all men have not faith. - 2 Thessalonians 3:1-2

So far, we have observed that the focus of prayer was woven around salvation, spiritual growth, and the course of the gospel. Worthy of note is the fact that praying for others was more prominent and consistent. This presupposes that beyond receiving things, prayer has now become a ministry to every believers.

[18]Praying always with all prayer and supplication in the Spirit, and watching thereunto with all perseverance and supplication for all saints;

[19]And for me, that utterance may be given unto me, that I may open my mouth boldly, to make known the mystery of the gospel,-

Ephesians 6:18-19

Every believer has a ministry of prayer to fellow believers and ministers. One of the ways believers are to serve each other in love is by praying for each other. Hence the Apostolic instructions to pray without ceasing, as there will never be a time when praying for other believers will be unnecessary. This further reinforces the fact that a believer's prayer life should not be reactionary.

Since God desires that all men be saved and come to the knowledge of the truth (spiritual growth), and since this desire cannot come to manifestation without the cooperation of believers, hence the responsibility of salvation (getting sinners saved via preaching) and spiritual growth, He has given to men (believers).

Every Believer has been given the ministry of reconciliation.

[17]Therefore if any man be in Christ, he is a new creature: old things are passed away; behold, all things are become new.

[18]And all things are of God, who hath reconciled us to himself by Jesus Christ, and hath given to us the ministry of reconciliation; - 2 Corinthians 5:17-18

[15]And he said unto them, Go ye into all the world, and preach the gospel to every creature. - Mark 16:15

[18]And Jesus came and spake unto them, saying, All power is given unto me in heaven and in earth.

[19]Go ye therefore, and teach all nations, baptizing them in the name of the Father, and of the Son, and of the Holy Ghost:

[20]Teaching them to observe all things whatsoever I have commanded you: and, lo, I am with you alway, even unto the end of the world. Amen. - Matthew 28:18-20

Every believer has been commissioned to preach, and teach the gospel to all nations, that is, to make disciples or student of all nations. This is how God's desire is fulfilled on the earth.

[28]Whom we preach, warning every man, and teaching every man in all wisdom; that we may present every man perfect in Christ Jesus: - Colossians 1:28

Man is responsible for presenting believers perfect (matured) in Christ Jesus, this explains that man is the one responsible for the spiritual growth of other believers.

Ephesians 4:11-13

[11]And he gave some, apostles; and some, prophets; and some, evangelists; and some, pastors and teachers;
[12]For the perfecting of the saints, for the work of the ministry, for the edifying of the body of Christ:

[13]Till we all come in the unity of the faith, and of the knowledge of the Son of God, unto a perfect man, unto the measure of the stature of the fulness of Christ: - Colossians 1:28

In light of this, the greatest priority of all believers should be the responsibility which God has given him and this should reflect in his prayer life.

All we have seen so far does not insinuate that it is wrong for believers ask for their personal needs in prayer. The Apostles, in their epistles, also give room for believers to ask for their personal desires in prayers however this was not as loud as praying for others.

[5]If any of you lack wisdom, let him ask of God, that giveth to all men liberally, and upbraideth not; and it shall be given him. - James 1:5

While the context of the text above was for those who are facing persecutions and trials, James admonished that if any lack wisdom and in this context, implies wisdom in handling persecutions, this however presupposes that when a believer lacks anything he can ask in prayer.

[14]And this is the confidence that we have in him, that, if we ***ask any thing****, according to his will he heareth us:*

[15]And if we know that he hear us, ***whatsoever we ask****, we know that we have the petitions that we desired of him.* - 1 John 5:14-15

Observe from the text above the phrase "ask anything" and "whatsoever we ask" both speak of our desires in prayer, which implies that the believer has the liberty to express his personal desires to God in prayers.

However, the Apostles were not so loud on this as they were on praying for fellow believers and ministers as we have earlier seen. Hence, this should take preeminence in our prayers also.

Let us examine **what Believers should pray for as revealed and instructed in the scriptures.**

1. The believers are to pray for the unsaved

[37]Then saith he unto his disciples, The harvest truly is plenteous, but the labourers are few;

[38]Pray ye therefore the Lord of the harvest, that he will send forth labourers into his harvest. - Matthew 9:37-38

In praying for the unsaved, we do not, necessarily, pray for them to be saved because for salvation to happen there has to be a preacher.

[13]For whosoever shall call upon the name of the Lord shall be saved.

[14]How then shall they call on him in whom they have not believed?

and how shall they believe in him of whom they have not heard? and how shall they hear without a preacher? - Romans 10:13-14

Hence, the believer is to pray for a preacher to be sent to the unsaved so the message of the gospel can get to them in case one cannot directly reach the person due to distance or other factors.

2. We pray for ourselves and fellow believers

[16]Cease not to give thanks for you, making mention of you in my prayers;

[17]That the God of our Lord Jesus Christ, the Father of glory, may give unto you the spirit of wisdom and revelation in the knowledge of him:

[18]The eyes of your understanding being enlightened; that ye may know what is the hope of his calling, and what the riches of the glory of his inheritance in the saints,

[19]And what is the exceeding greatness of his power to us-ward who believe, according to the working of his mighty power,

[20]Which he wrought in Christ, when he raised him from the dead, and set him at his own right hand in the heavenly places,

[21]Far above all principality, and power, and might, and dominion, and every name that is named, not only in this world, but also in that which is to come: - Ephesians 1:16-21

i. In praying for ourselves, and fellow believers, we are to pray for insight into God's word and the power at work in us.

ii. We also pray for strengthening by the spirit within, and a comprehension of the love of Christ.

[14]For this cause I bow my knees unto the Father of our Lord Jesus Christ,

[15]Of whom the whole family in heaven and earth is named,

[16]That he would grant you, according to the riches of his glory, to be strengthened with might by his Spirit in the inner man;

[17]That Christ may dwell in your hearts by faith; that ye, being rooted and grounded in love,

[18]May be able to comprehend with all saints what is the breadth, and length, and depth, and height;

[19]And to know the love of Christ, which passeth knowledge, that ye might be filled with all the fulnessPh God. - Ephesians 3:14-19

iii. We can also pray that our love walk will abound more in knowledge and in all judgement; that we will be sincere and without offence till the day of Christ

[9]And this I pray, that your love may abound yet more and more in knowledge and in all judgment;

[10]That ye may approve things that are excellent; that ye may be sincere and without offence till the day of Christ; - Philippians 1:9-10

iv. We can also pray that we will be full of knowledge to appreciate and walk in God's plan and purposes, so we please him, producing fruits and thus strengthened.

[9]For this cause we also, since the day we heard it, do not cease to pray for you, and to desire that ye might be filled with the knowledge of his will in all wisdom and spiritual understanding;

[10]That ye might walk worthy of the Lord unto all pleasing, being fruitful in every good work, and increasing in the knowledge of God;

[11]Strengthened with all might, according to his glorious power, unto all patience and longsuffering with joyfulness; - Colossians 1:9-11

[20]Now the God of peace, that brought again from the dead our Lord Jesus, that great shepherd of the sheep, through the blood of the everlasting covenant,

[21]Make you perfect in every good work to do his will, working in

you that which is wellpleasing in his sight, through Jesus Christ; to whom be glory for ever and ever. Amen. - Hebrews 13:20-21

v. We are to pray that the sharing of our faith becomes more effective through our knowledge of Christ.

[4]Always in every prayer of mine for you all making request with joy,

[5]For your fellowship in the gospel from the first day until now;

[6]Being confident of this very thing, that he which hath begun a good work in you will perform it until the day of Jesus Christ: - Philippians 1:4-6

vi. We are to pray that we stand complete and perfect in all the will of God.

[12]Epaphras, who is one of you, a servant of Christ, saluteth you, always labouring fervently for you in prayers, that ye may stand perfect and complete in all the will of God. - Colossians 4:12

vii. We are to pray that we will be worthy of our calling by fulfilling his will, and the effect of our faith (knowledge) and Jesus is glorified.

[11]Wherefore also we pray always for you, that our God would count you worthy of this calling, and fulfil all the good pleasure of his goodness, and the work of faith with power:

[12]That the name of our Lord Jesus Christ may be glorified in you, and ye in him, according to the grace of our God and the Lord Jesus Christ. - 2 Thessalonians 1:11-12

Observe all of these prayers focuse on knowledge. This is because spiritual growth is growth in the knowledge of our salvation, hence, the most important thing a believer needs is knowledge. In all situations, circumstances and times, the believers need will always be knowledge. So, we must not allow our emotions dictate to us how we should pray, rather we should pray as instructed and led by the written word.

3. We are to also pray for ministers of the Gospel

[18]Praying always with all prayer and supplication in the Spirit, and watching thereunto with all perseverance and supplication for all saints;

[19]And for me, that utterance may be given unto me, that I may open my mouth boldly, to make known the mystery of the gospel,

[20]For which I am an ambassador in bonds: that therein I may speak boldly, as I ought to speak. - Ephesians 6:18-20

The instruction to pray for all saints (believers) also includes ministers (Pastors and leaders in the church).

i. We are to pray that utterance be given to them, and that they will boldly declare the Gospel as they should.

[2]Continue in prayer, and watch in the same with thanksgiving; - Colossians 4:2

[29]And now, Lord, behold their threatenings: and grant unto thy servants, that with all boldness they may speak thy word, - Acts 4:29

ii. We are to also pray for their deliverance, preservation, and that their ministry will be received.

[30]Now I beseech you, brethren, for the Lord Jesus Christ's sake, and for the love of the Spirit, that ye strive together with me in your prayers to God for me; - Romans 15:30

[1]Finally, brethren, pray for us, that the word of the Lord may have free course, and be glorified, even as it is with you:

[2]And that we may be delivered from unreasonable and wicked men: for all men have not faith. - 2 Thessalonians 3:1-2

iii. We are also to pray that signs, and wonders be done in their ministry

[28]For to do whatsoever thy hand and thy counsel determined before to be done.

[29]And now, Lord, behold their threatenings: and grant unto thy servants, that with all boldness they may speak thy word,

[30]By stretching forth thine hand to heal; and that signs and wonders may be done by the name of thy holy child Jesus. - Acts 4:28-30

iv. We are also to pray that their conscience, and conduct be pleasing to God.

[18]Pray for us: for we trust we have a good conscience, in all things willing to live honestly. - Hebrews 13:18

4. As believers, we must understand that the local church is God's wisdom to mature us spiritually. By its activities, the believer is brought to that place of maturity (we have examined this, exhaustively, in the previous chapter). If the local church, and its activities/meetings are important for christian growth, then such meetings must be taken, and regarded as sacred and important. Hence, we are required to prayerfully prepare our hearts to receive in such meeting.

Again, if we can pray for fellow believers, and ministers, then we can pray concerning Christian meetings too. As important as planning and strategies are important in preparing for Christian meetings, it must not replace the place of prayer. Christian meetings are supernatural, and should not be treated as secular meeting.

In prayers we make power available ahead of the meetings, and the reason for the gathering is optimally achieved.

[16]Confess your faults one to another, and pray one for another, that ye may be healed. The effectual fervent prayer of a righteous man availeth much. - James 5:16

Having seen this, what then do we need to pray for in preparation of christian meetings? Firstly, we shouldn't be found praying for the presence of God to be in the meeting because that will be unbelief. The word of God already revealed that when believers are gathered, the power of the Lord Jesus is gathered with them.

[4]In the name of our Lord Jesus Christ, when ye are gathered together, and my spirit, with the power of our Lord Jesus Christ, - 1 Corinthians 5:4

Also believers are temple of the spirit and as result have the presence of God with them wherever they go

[16]Know ye not that ye are the temple of God, and that the Spirit of God dwelleth in you? - 1 Corinthians 3:16

To recognize what to pray for in preparing for christian meetings, we must first understand that the primary reason believers gather is to be edified, and be built up. In this, the believer becomes more effective in his Christian walk.

[26]How is it then, brethren? when ye come together, every one of you hath a psalm, hath a doctrine, hath a tongue, hath a revelation, hath an interpretation. ***Let all things be done unto edifying.*** - 1 Corinthians 14:26

From the text above we can deduce that everyone in the gathering; the ministers and members alike, are responsible for edifying others as well as they are to receive edification from others.

[11]And he gave some, apostles; and some, prophets; and some, evangelists; and some, pastors and teachers;

[12]For the perfecting of the saints, for the work of the ministry, for the edifying of the body of Christ - Ephesians 4:11-12

The essence of the ministry gifts are to mature the saints to the end that they are effective in the work of the ministry, and consequently given for the edifying of the body. Therefore, it suffices to say that both the ministers (pastors & leaders), and members do the edifying in a Christian meeting, hence, they are the ones to be prayed for.

i. For ministers, we pray for utterance and boldness.

[3]Withal praying also for us, that God would open unto us a door of utterance, to speak the mystery of Christ, for which I am also in bonds:

[4]That I may make it manifest, as I ought to speak. - Colossians 4:3-4

[19]And for me, that utterance may be given unto me, that I may open my mouth boldly, to make known the mystery of the gospel,

[20]For which I am an ambassador in bonds: that therein I may speak boldly, as I ought to speak. - Ephesians 6:19-20

[30]By stretching forth thine hand to heal; and that signs and wonders may be done by the name of thy holy child Jesus.

[31]And when they had prayed, the place was shaken where they were assembled together; and they were all filled with the Holy Ghost, and they spake the word of God with boldness - Acts 4:30-31

ii. For the participants, we pray for insight into God's word to the end that they are edified.

Eph 1:17-23, 3:14-21, Phil 1:9-12, Col 1:9-11

5. We pray that those handling natural responsibilities(non preaching assignments), during the meeting, receive wisdom.

[5]If any of you lack wisdom, let him ask of God, that giveth to all men liberally, and upbraideth not; and it shall be given him.- James 1:5

Wisdom was a primary requirement in choosing deacons to serve tables in the early church.

[3]Wherefore, brethren, look ye out among you seven men of honest report, full of the Holy Ghost and wisdom, whom we may appoint over this business. - Acts 6:3

We also pray that they receive wisdom to the end that they may have all things done and attended to decently and in order.

[40]Let all things be done decently and in order. - 1 Corinthians 14:40

6. We can also pray specifically for situations that surround such meetings like good weather, oppositions, supernatural publicity, financial supply or resources etc.

There's a popular quote by Charles Spurgeon that says "when asked what is more important; praying or reading the Bible? I ask what is more important; breathing in or breathing out". This emphasizes the necessity of these two activities in our Christian walk. A believer must seek to build a strong personal culture of prayer and study of the word if he must be effective in his walk with the Lord.

CONCLUSION

Christianity is a supernatural life. It is the life of the Spirit, in the believer as we have since examined.

In the New birth, Eternal life is received by the Spirit in the believer.

[3] According as his divine power hath given unto us all things that pertain unto life and godliness, through the knowledge of him that hath called us to glory and virtue:

[4] Whereby are given unto us exceeding great and precious promises: that by these ye might be partakers of the divine nature, having escaped the corruption that is in the world through lust.- 2 Peter 1:3-4

The believer is a partaker of God's divine nature. In the new birth, he shares of the life, and nature of God; he has received supernatural abilities, God's character, amongst others. Hence, Paul taught that God is the one working in the believer both to will, and to do his good pleasure.

[13] For it is God which worketh in you both to will and to do of his good pleasure. - Philippians 2:13

Christianity is a demonstration of a higher life, at work in the believer. It is first received, then expressed afterwards. Hence instructions, in the written word, for believers, are first a revelation of what he can do (his abilities). God has not told the believer to do what he has not been enabled for.

[25] If we live in the Spirit, let us also walk in the Spirit. - Galatians 5:25

Paul's instructions, here, suggest an expression, and not a performance. The Christian conduct is not a performance, it is an expression of the life of the Spirit (God) in the believer.

Paul had earlier spoken of the result (fruit) of the Spirit in the believer.

[22] But the fruit of the Spirit is love, joy, peace, longsuffering, gentleness, goodness, faith,

[23] Meekness, temperance: against such there is no law. - Galatians 5:22-23

All the fruits of the Spirit, in the believer, are his characters; the believer is born with them (Ephesians 2:10). To act otherwise will be to live a lie. Spiritual maturity is explained, in scripture, in this light. It is not an attempt to become anything more other than what the believer is, rather, it is an effectiveness that comes by the believer's revelation and constant focus on his identity in Christ; the new life, status, and possessions that he has in Christ. (James 1: 22-25, Philemon 1:6, 2 Peter 3:18)

Ministry is also explained in this light.

[11] And he gave some, apostles; and some, prophets; and some, evangelists; and some, pastors and teachers;

[12] For the perfecting of the saints, for the work of the ministry, for the edifying of the body of Christ:

[13] Till we all come in the unity of the faith, and of the knowledge of the Son of God, unto a perfect man, unto the measure of the stature of the fulness of Christ - Ephesians 4:11-13

From the text above, it is crystal clear that ministry gifts in the local church are to bring the saints to a place of maturity for ministry. This implies that all believers have a calling into the ministry of Christ, and spiritual maturity will be revealed in the believer's participation in the work of the ministry.

[17] Therefore if any man be in Christ, he is a new creature: old things are passed away; behold, all things are become new.

[18] And all things are of God, who hath reconciled us to himself by Jesus Christ, and hath given to us the ministry of reconciliation; - 2 Corinthians 5:17-18

The text above further affirms that the work of ministry is every believer's responsibility. Notice that the same believer that's referred to as a new creation in verse 17, is the same one who has been given the ministry of reconciliation in verse 18. This would mean that at salvation, every believer has been given the ministry, and responsibility to preach the gospel.

[9] But ye are a chosen generation, a royal priesthood, an holy nation, a peculiar people; that ye should shew forth the praises of him who hath called you out of darkness into his marvellous light:- 1 Peter 2:9

Peter further affirms, here, that the purpose of the new birth is ministry/service. In the new birth, believers receive the Spirit by which he is regenerated and made a new creation (Titus 3:5, 1 Corinthians 6:11). However, the Spirit received at salvation is how God consecrates and enabled the believer for the work of ministry; just like how Moses, in the Old Testament, appointed, and consecrated vessels for service in the temple.

In the New birth, the new creation man is enriched with the abilities required for service/ministry

[4] I thank my God always for you because of the grace of God which was given you in Christ Jesus,

[5] so that in everything you were [exceedingly] enriched in Him, in all speech [empowered by the spiritual gifts] and in all knowledge [with insight into the faith].

[6]In this way our testimony about Christ was confirmed and established in you,

[7]so that you are not lacking in any spiritual gift [which comes from the Holy Spirit], as you eagerly wait [with confident trust] for the revelation of our Lord Jesus Christ [when He returns]. - 1 Corinthians 1:4-7 (Amplified)

[7] But the manifestation of the Spirit is given to every man to profit withal. - 1 Corinthians 12:7

The word manifestation here implies an unveiling, a full disclosure, it refers to the giving of the Spirit. The believer received the full disclosure of the Spirit in the new birth.

Apostle Paul taught that the Spirit received in the new birth is for ministry, it is profit or serve the kingdom purpose.

Paul in latter verses now revealed certain supernatural abilities residence in that Spirit which the believer received in the New birth.

[8] For to one is given by the Spirit the word of wisdom; to another the word of knowledge by the

same Spirit;

[9] To another faith by the same Spirit; to another the gifts of healing by the same Spirit;

[10] To another the working of miracles; to another prophecy; to another discerning of spirits; to another divers kinds of tongues; to another the interpretation of tongues: - 1 Corinthians 12:8-10

This diversities of gifts Paul mentioned are in the Spirit in the believer, thus the believer have all of them, since he has the Spirit thus Paul instructed that he can desire or covet the best gift (1 Corinthians 12:31; 14:12)

That said, By the Spirit in the believer from salvation, the believer have the ability to;

1. Speak by the Spirit (Utterance gift - Tongues, Interpretation, Prophecy)

2. See and know by the Spirit (Revelation gift - a word of knowledge, a word of wisdom, discerning of spirit)

3. To do by the Spirit (Power gift - gift of healings, gift of working of miracles, gift of faith)

All these are a function of the New birth, hence the believer is born with the gifts of the Spirit. The gifts of the Spirit will be found in the New birth.

Before a child speaks, that child is born with the ability to speak, a baby will see because he have the eyes to see, he is born with the ability to see which is the eyes, so is the believer also, he will speak with tongues and exudes supernatural abilities because he has the ability to, however an ignorance believer can be crippled in his participation in the gifts in the Spirit. The day a believer begins to practice his gifts in the Spirit is necessarily not the day he received the ability, but the day he find out or become willing because the ability are inherent since the new birth. All these will be further explained in details in the next volume of this book.

The gifts of the Spirit are residence in every believer from the point of salvation for ministry. This further affirm that the work of ministry is not a special call for a special people rather every believer have been called and are to be subjected to training in their local church for Ministry. This was the practice in the early church except for Paul's case who had an encounter with Jesus on his way to Damascus (Acts 9:1-16), however, Paul still had to identify with the disciples in Jerusalem.

[19] And when he had received meat, he was strengthened. Then was Saul certain days with the disciples which were at Damascus.

[26] And when Saul was come to Jerusalem, he assayed to join himself to the disciples: but they were all afraid of him, and believed not that he was a disciple.

[27] But Barnabas took him, and brought him to the apostles, and declared unto them how he had seen the Lord in the way, and that he had spoken to him, and how he had preached boldly at Damascus in the name of Jesus.

[28] And he was with them coming in and going out at Jerusalem. - Acts 9:19,26-28

There are other instances in the book of Acts, where believers went through the process of discipleship till they assume oversight functions and responsibilities over other believers. Such is the case of the twelve disciples of Jesus, who later became the Apostles in the early church, except Judas Iscariot.

Some of Apostle Paul's converts & disciples (in Acts 19), eventually became the elders who now oversaw other believers in the church.

[27] For I have not shunned to declare unto you all the counsel of God.

[28] Take heed therefore unto yourselves, and to all the flock, over the which the Holy Ghost hath made you overseers, to feed the church

of God, which he hath purchased with his own blood.

[29] For I know this, that after my departing shall grievous wolves enter in among you, not sparing the flock.

[30] Also of your own selves shall men arise, speaking perverse things, to draw away disciples after them.

[31] Therefore watch, and remember, that by the space of three years I ceased not to warn every one night and day with tears.

[32] And now, brethren, I commend you to God, and to the word of his grace, which is able to build you up, and to give you an inheritance among all them which are sanctified. - Acts 20:27-32

That said, another important fact to consider as we conclude this study is Jesus instruction to his disciple before his ascension.

[15] And he said unto them, Go ye into all the world, and preach the gospel to every creature.

[16] He that believeth and is baptized shall be saved; but he that believeth not shall be damned. [17] And these signs shall follow them that believe; In my name shall they cast out devils; they shall speak with new tongues;

[18] They shall take up serpents; and if they drink any deadly thing, it shall not hurt them; they shall lay hands on the sick, and they shall recover. - Mark 16:15-18

Luke was more detailed in his account;

[45] Then opened he their understanding, that they might understand the scriptures,

[46] And said unto them, Thus it is written, and thus it behoved Christ to suffer, and to rise from the dead the third day:

[47] And that repentance and remission of sins should be preached in his name among all nations, beginning at Jerusalem.

[48] And ye are witnesses of these things.

[49] And, behold, I send the promise of my Father upon you: but

tarry ye in the city of Jerusalem, until ye be endued with power from on high. - Luke 24:45-49

Jesus, upon instructing his disciples to preach forgiveness of sins (the gospel), told them to wait for the promise of the father and we saw the fulfillment of this on the day of Pentecost.

Peter explained the event as the fulfillment of the promise of God Joel spoke of in Joel 2:28-29.

[16] But this is that which was spoken by the prophet Joel;

[17] And it shall come to pass in the last days, saith God, I will pour out of my Spirit upon all flesh: and your sons and your daughters shall prophesy, and your young men shall see visions, and your old men shall dream dreams:

[18] And on my servants and on my handmaidens I will pour out in those days of my Spirit; and they shall prophesy: - Acts 2:16-18

Notice, the phrase "pour out of my Spirit" refers to an outpouring from the Spirit of the believer quite different from Ezekiel's prophecy which is an indwelling. Joel's prophecy is built on Ezekiel's.

Jesus referred to the event of the day of Pentecost as fulfillment of John's message.

[4] And, being assembled together with them, commanded them that they should not depart from Jerusalem, but wait for the promise of the Father, which, saith he, ye have heard of me.

[5] For John truly baptized with water; but ye shall be baptized with the Holy Ghost not many days hence. - Acts 1:4-5

John the Baptist called it to be Baptized with the Holyghost or

Holyghost Baptism.

On the day of Pentecost, there was a shedding forth from the believers to others; tongues, prophecy amongst other demonstrations of the Spirit. However, the most notable thing was that Peter preached the gospel and 3000 souls got born again, were added to the church, and continued in the Apostles teachings. This is the purpose of "Pentecost" or the Baptism of the Holy ghost, it is for ministry.

Subsequently, from that day, in the Apostles' (the church) evangelistic outreaches, as soon as their audience received the word, they got them filled with the Holyghost with the evidence of speaking with tongues;

[5] Then Philip went down to the city of Samaria, and preached Christ unto them.

[6] And the people with one accord gave heed unto those things which Philip spake, hearing and seeing the miracles which he did.

[12] But when they believed Philip preaching the things concerning the kingdom of God, and the name of Jesus Christ, they were baptized, both men and women.

[14] Now when the apostles which were at Jerusalem heard that Samaria had received the word of God, they sent unto them Peter and John:

[15] Who, when they were come down, prayed for them, that they might receive the Holy Ghost:

[16] (For as yet he was fallen upon none of them: only they were baptized in the name of the Lord Jesus.)

[17] Then laid they their hands on them, and they received the Holy Ghost.- Acts 8:5-6,12,14-17

Samaria received the word (the gospel) and were prayed for to receive the Holy ghost

[34] Then Peter opened his mouth, and said, Of a truth I perceive that God is no respecter of persons:

[37] That word, I say, ye know, which was published throughout all Judaea, and began from Galilee, after the baptism which John preached;

[38] How God anointed Jesus of Nazareth with the Holy Ghost and with power: who went about doing good, and healing all that were oppressed of the devil; for God was with him.

[39] And we are witnesses of all things which he did both in the land of the Jews, and in Jerusalem; whom they slew and hanged on a tree:

[40] Him God raised up the third day, and shewed him openly;

[41] Not to all the people, but unto witnesses chosen before of God, even to us, who did eat and drink with him after he rose from the dead.

[42] And he commanded us to preach unto the people, and to testify that it is he which was ordained of God to be the Judge of quick and dead.

[43] To him give all the prophets witness, that through his name whosoever believeth in him shall receive remission of sins.

[44] While Peter yet spake these words, the Holy Ghost fell on all them which heard the word.

[45] And they of the circumcision which believed were astonished, as many as came with Peter, because that on the Gentiles also was poured out the gift of the Holy Ghost.

[46] For they heard them speak with tongues, and magnify God. Then answered Peter, - Acts 10:34,37-46

The household of Cornelius had the gospel preached to him and they responded with faith in their heart and while Peter was still preaching, they got filled with the holy ghost and began to speak with tongues and magnify God

[1] And it came to pass, that, while Apollos was at Corinth, Paul having passed through the upper coasts came to Ephesus: and finding certain disciples,

[2] He said unto them, Have ye received the Holy Ghost since ye believed? And they said unto him, We have not so much as heard whether there be any Holy Ghost.

[3] And he said unto them, Unto what then were ye baptized? And they said, Unto John's baptism. [4] Then said Paul, John verily baptized with the baptism of repentance, saying unto the people, that they should believe on him which should come after him, that is, on Christ Jesus.

[5] When they heard this, they were baptized in the name of the Lord Jesus.

[6] And when Paul had laid his hands upon them, the Holy Ghost came on them; and they spake with tongues, and prophesied. - Acts 19:1-6

Paul having preached the gospel to this ignorant disciple, they believed and had him laid on hands on them to receive the Holy ghost. This will presuppose that;

1. The Baptism of the Holyghost, with the evidence of tongues, is for every believer.

2. This should follow salvation, believers ought to be filled with the Spirit immediately after salvation.

3. Since we established that the baptism of the Holyghost is for ministry, it implies that as they were getting new converts, they were getting baptized with the Holyghost for ministry which further affirm that every believer has been called to do ministry.

The salvation experience is all the qualification required to be filled with the Spirit. Recall that we have earlier established that tongues is an inherent ability of the believer in salvation.

The ability did not come when the Apostles prayed, because God plays the exclusive role of giving man the Spirit wherein lies all these supernatural abilities (Ezekiel 36:25-27). No man can give the Spirit.

However, When prayers are made for believers to receive the Holy Ghost, it is to help him to take from the abilities already within. Hence, Joel in his prophecy called it "God pouring of His Spirit upon all flesh". God does that from the Spirit in the believer; tongues, prophecy and others. Hence, the Holyghost baptism, otherwise known as the outpouring of the Spirit, is for every believer and we should all desire it.

Having read through this book, I trust that you have been blessed and that your mind has been opened to the basic, yet, important truths you should know about the practice of Christianity; how that our effectiveness as believers greatly hinges on our appreciation of this unchangeable truth of Christianity. There are yet many other facts of Christianity you should be informed about as a believer. I therefore urge you to ensure that you get the volume 2 of this book.

tongues is an inherent ability of the believer in salvation.

[illegible] they did [illegible] and [illegible] received [illegible] they [illegible] could [illegible] the Spirit, where [illegible] these [illegible] (Acts 10:[illegible]) [illegible]

However, [illegible] prayer [illegible] needed for believers to receive the Holy [illegible] it is [illegible] from the [illegible] already within. [illegible] Joel in his prophecy called it "God's pouring of His Spirit upon all flesh." God [illegible] that [illegible] the Spirit in the believer [illegible] and [illegible] the Holy Ghost [illegible] what the [illegible] of the Spirit is for every believer and we should all desire it.

Having read through this book, I trust that you have been blessed and that your [illegible] has been opened to the basic, yet important truths [illegible] should know [illegible] the [illegible] of Christianity [illegible] that [illegible] believer's [illegible] of [illegible] yet [illegible] Christianity, you [illegible] about as a believer. [illegible] encourage you to [illegible] this book.

www.ingramcontent.com/pod-product-compliance
Lightning Source LLC
LaVergne TN
LVHW012057160826
845678LV00014B/2858